REASONS FOR FAITH

Oliver R Barclay

Reasons for Faith

Inter-Varsity Press

©INTER-VARSITY PRESS, LONDON

Inter-Varsity Fellowship
39 Bedford Square
London WC1B 3EY

First edition May 1974

ISBN 0 85110 376 6

Printed in Great Britain by
Hunt Barnard Printing Ltd, Aylesbury, Bucks.

Contents

Preface

Many people think of Christian faith as similar to a virus infection such as 'flu. Either you have caught it or you haven't. There is very little you can do about it either way. Some people are susceptible and some aren't. It may go in epidemics or it may die out. To some extent you can try to avoid infection, or you can expose yourself to it; but that is all. There is no logic about it. It just happens to some people and not to others. To those who hold that view (and to some others) this book will seem to be a mistake. There are both non-Christians and some Christians who would think that what I am doing is a misguided, or at least a too dangerous, endeavour. Obviously I do not share that view and it may be worth while to say why.

First, I believe that it is very important to say again today that the Christian faith is to be believed primarily because it happens to be true. We do not believe because it is comforting, increases psychological health or international peace, or seems to us attractive and pleasant for any other reason. But if people are to believe that it is true, they must be helped to think about it and to see *why* it is held to be true.

Secondly, the New Testament evangelists, including the apostles, seem to me to have believed in and practised this kind of approach. In many situations they *argued* for the existence and nature of the Creator, the deity of Christ and the reality of Christian experience as a work of the Holy Spirit. If that is a right estimate of their method it is by itself enough justification for our making the effort to do the same. Indeed it suggests that it is a positive duty. In this book I have tried, with some care, to argue as they did and to give to human reason the same kind of place that they did. The reader must judge whether I have succeeded.

Thirdly, the New Testament tells us that Christians should be ready always to give a reason for the hope that is in them. The apostles were willing to come down into the market places and debating halls and discuss with all who would meet with them. We must be ready and prepared for such discussion too. This book is intended to be that kind of a discussion with the non-Christian and may incidentally serve to prepare Christians for similar discussion.

On the other side some will argue that the attempt betrays a too intellectual view of faith, or that such discussion easily creates a false confidence in human reasoning, leaving the truth at the mercy of the most clever arguments of the day. We are in danger, therefore, of detracting from the wonder of God's initiative in making himself known to men. I accept that there are dangers; but we must be ruled by the teaching and example of the apostles. Direct preaching evangelism is also subject to parallel dangers but we do not for that reason stop preaching. We must not be too influenced by current fashions. Twentieth-century philosophical trends are a bad guide to what Christianity should be like.

Paul in his short address to a pagan audience at Lystra, which is recorded in Acts 14, says of the pattern of the world that 'God did not leave himself without witness'. Basically what I hope to do is to *bear witness* to those main truths about God that he has been pleased to give us. Christians bear witness to the fact of a Creator; they bear witness to a divine Saviour, Jesus Christ; they also bear witness to the fact that God the Holy Spirit is active in the lives of his people. These truths all converge to confront us with God and with our need to respond to him. The Christian's responsibility is witness. It is God who can open men's minds and wills to accept the truth. The reader's responsibility is to try to deal honestly and critically with the material set before him.

I owe it to many people to acknowledge their help, not least to the many non-Christian students who have discussed these things with me over the years. My wife deserves special mention for her encouragement and suggestions, and for the very formidable work of typing the manuscript. My thanks are also particularly due to those who made it possible for me to have some time away from my usual job so that I could start putting this book together. Without that it is most unlikely that it would ever have been written.

Introduction: Reasons for faith

When Galileo developed his revolutionary ideas about the solar system he invited the professors from the University of Padua to come and look through his telescope. The Professor of Philosophy refused. That seems to us disgraceful but to a philosopher of the early 17th century what one might see through some new-fangled instrument seemed irrelevant. If you wanted to know about the movements of the heavenly bodies the answer was to be found in the thinking of the great wise men. That sort of problem was solved by reading Aristotle and other great thinkers of the previous two thousand years. The Professor of Philosophy was never convinced and continued to the end of his life to believe that the earth was the centre of the solar system and the heavenly bodies all moved round the earth in a complex pattern of perfect circles. He and others were never convinced because they refused to come and see for themselves and they refused to come and see because they thought it was a silly way to solve a problem. One of Galileo's opponents wrote of his discoveries: 'Nature abhors such horrible chaos, and to the truly wise such variety is detestable.'

Galileo on the other hand represents a more scientific outlook. He had been shaken out of the almost universally accepted opinion by two things. First, he had an open and inquisitive mind, so he had played around with several alternative views of the matter. Secondly, he had come upon some new facts of observation which made the old views extremely difficult to maintain. He concluded that the earth moved round the sun. Hardly anyone supported him; so he wanted them to come and examine the data for themselves and think out with him whether his new theories were convincing or not.

Many people have seen in this incident the heart of the conflict between science and religion. That is not really correct. The conflict was between two methods; between relying on philosophical reasoning and tradition on the one hand and relying on a fresh look at the facts on the other. Theology and philosophy in Galileo's day emphasized the first. Science is one of the disciplines that emphasizes the second method and the debate is still with us. Today, however, the rôles have often been reversed. Many people dismiss Christianity without examining it. They may or may not be scientists, but they do not go into the question of the truth of Christianity because they are settled in their own outlook and, like the philosophers of Padua, they refuse to come and see. The Christian is more often in the position of Galileo. Against the majority opinion and a substantial array of theoretical arguments he claims that the facts, if rightly understood, would lead one to see that Christianity is true. The Christian not only presents facts, however, though that is as basic as it is for science. He also tries to show people what they mean. He has to invite people to come and see for themselves and to discuss the meaning of what they see. This book is a contribution to that task.

The New Testament writers assert three main grounds for belief. First, they assert that men do have some knowledge of the Creator from what they see of his creation. Secondly they point to the figure of Jesus Christ and state that he can be rightly seen only as more than man – indeed as God come in love to rescue man. Thirdly they assert that God is active in the lives of many ordinary men and women and that there is evidence here too that in life we have to deal, not with impersonal or social forces only, but with the living God. This book will approach the data in terms of these three divisions.

The Christian God is after all not merely the 'force' behind the universe, though he is that. He is not merely the 'ground of our being', though in some respects that is a use-

12

ful way to think of him. The Christian God makes himself known as the eternal Creator, the historically incarnate Son and the present living reality of the Holy Spirit in his people. I want to try to show that God speaks to us in all these ways. I shall not discuss the doctrine of the Trinity. I want to let the facts speak for themselves and tell us different things about the one personal, eternal, living God.

It is important to point out that there are two broadly different kinds of reasons for faith. They can be called reasons from inside and reasons from outside. Some arguments for Christianity are only really effective when they are part of the whole Christian picture of reality. These are the reasons from inside. In that context they help to show that Christianity is consistent and convincing as a whole. I believe that the argument about evil can be dealt with only in this way. In this book, however, I shall try to emphasize the reasons from outside, that is to say the reasons that stand more easily on their own, and begin with some sort of common ground between Christian and non-Christian. This common ground is what I refer to as the data or the facts.

Before starting to discuss data, however, we want to explain our approach. We are not going to present the philosophical 'proofs' for God, though we shall to some extent overlap with some of those arguments. We are not trying to establish a rationally demonstrated 'uncaused cause', or 'tendency that works for righteousness', or any other intellectual abstraction, and then claim that this is God. Such a path can lead only to belief in a highly abstract kind of God. Our method is determined by the nature of Christian faith, which we must first define.

What is faith?

Christian faith is not merely believing that certain things 'are the case'. That view of faith was popular for a time but is rightly discredited today. Even back in the New Testament itself one writer points out somewhat scathingly that the

13

devils believe 'that there is one God' – and tremble. The devils of course do absolutely nothing about it. That sort of believing is dismissed as worthless and we have no difficulty in agreeing with that judgment. Today the tendency is more often to swing to the other extreme and to think of faith as an almost irrational leap in the dark to which no kind of reasoning could make any real contribution.

What then is the Christian's view of faith? The trouble is that faith is one of those words – like love or understanding – that is very much altered by its object. If I say that I have faith in a formula or a cooking recipe I am describing something quite different from what I mean when I say that I have faith in my wife. Christian faith is at least faith in a personal God. Its essence is *trust*. It is often spoken of as trust in Jesus Christ. It is best defined as trust in the God who is revealed and personified in Jesus Christ. Christian faith is therefore far richer than mere intellectual belief. It has vital aspects which such belief lacks. But equally it is based on truth. It cannot be a leap in the dark. Even less can it be believing what you think is probably false. In so far as it involves a leap it will be a leap in the light – a response to what we now see to be true. Men trust Christ when they are convinced that he is trustworthy and that their previous independence of him has been wrong. They cannot be asked to trust without such a foundation.

My task in this book, therefore, is to bring forward facts which provide a basis for trust in God. They lead us to the water, though they cannot make us drink. That is inevitable if faith is trust. But although facts cannot make us trust it is no good exhorting people to believe in someone whom they really do not think exists or to trust in Christ as God when they think he is a mere man. We need grounds for believing that Christianity is true before we can honestly trust in God. Our approach is therefore nearer to that of the scientist than to that of the philosopher. We want to present data and to show that they provide a basis for faith, however surprising and theoretically unlikely that may seem.

If a couple are considering marriage they are extremely foolish if they decide the matter merely on the basis of their feelings. If they are sensible they will make efforts to get to know one another. They will try to understand the home background, the standards of value, the likes and dislikes and all the other things that go to make up what a person is and what they are like to live with. At the same time all the understanding that they could have would be no real basis for marriage unless there was mutual trust and love. But trust must feed on knowledge of the person being trusted, and grows, or diminishes, as we know them better.

It is the same with Christian faith. While it is something far richer than mere intellectual assent, it feeds on facts about God. The facts need to be considered critically and also as honestly as we can. Faith depends on knowledge, not on ignorance. That is why I have called this book *Reasons for Faith*.

Faith and the will

This nature of faith means that we have to take note of one particular danger. We can easily be influenced by totally illogical factors. That, of course, is true also even in purely academic subjects. It is not easy to be impartial with the data, especially if you need to complete the essay quickly and want to present a nice and convincing story! Even in the school science lab the graphs we produced often showed tidier curves than the facts justified! It is extremely easy, without conscious dishonesty, to ignore inconvenient facts and come to the conclusions we want. If this is true in small matters it is even more true when the whole orientation of our life is at stake. If someone very much wants not to believe, all the evidence in the world will probably not convince him. If he wants to believe he may be far too uncritical in his original assessment and then run into difficulties afterwards. In any case Christian faith involves the will as well as the mind because it is trust.

None of us is altogether impartial and we may as well admit it at the start. What we need first of all, then, is to be genuinely open to the truth whatever it may turn out to be. God is not playing hide and seek with us. If he is there he is going to make himself known in due time to those who honestly seek, as Jesus explicitly promised. Meanwhile we must be on our guard against both wishful thinking and wishful unthinking while we try to look afresh at the relevant data. We want to know the truth and God (if there is a God like the Christian God) wants us to know the truth.

The reasons for faith that we want to bring forward are of two kinds. First, there are facts about the world, about Jesus Christ and about experience which need to be set out and considered. Then there are interpretations of these facts which will sometimes be in the form: this all makes sense in a Christian framework while no other framework can really explain it satisfactorily.

The position is not altogether unlike that of Galileo, only here we are talking about a personal God who speaks to us and not a bare mathematical theory. To the many who opposed Galileo he answered, first, that he had facts to show — both old ones reconsidered and some new telescopic data. Secondly, he suggested that all the data concerned were best understood in terms of a set of new overall concepts about the heavenly bodies. Some dared not follow him for fear of the opposition that might follow. Some were convinced, and some needed further time to go over the arguments again.

It is the same with Christianity. First we need to be exposed to, or reminded of, the relevant facts. Then we need to try to see what they signify – to ask ourselves what is the explanation of the facts? Here we have to look honestly at how other people see them. If we are driven in the end to accept the Christian estimate of God, then the only honest and right final step is to trust him. Faith comes in different ways but its basis is a realization that its foundation is true. There is a God like that and therefore we ought to trust him and can with confidence do so.

The plan is as follows. The book is divided into three parts. The first is concerned with the evidence that there is a Creator God. Part Two looks at the reasons for believing that the Creator God has revealed himself and his nature and plans for men in Jesus Christ. Part Three is concerned to show that the same living God is active in the world today. A concluding chapter seeks to draw these threads together.

Part One
God the Creator

1. Is the universe a creation?

There is a story of a Hyde Park orator who was attacking all ideas of belief in God and declaring that the world just happened without any personal or intelligent agent being responsible. As he spoke a rather soft tomato sailed through the air suspiciously close to his head. 'Who threw that?' he demanded angrily and a small Cockney voice from the back of the crowd replied: 'No-one. It threw itself.' Now it is just possible that it was purely accidental. Someone, perhaps, had sat on one end of a plank which tipped up violently and see-sawed it into the air. It may even be that by molecular bombardment an exceedingly rare combination of factors projected it just at that moment. In that case this very rare happening was really worthy of immediate scientific examination (was the tomato hot, for instance?). But whatever the *possible* scientific explanation the combination of events left no-one in any doubt that in fact someone had thrown it deliberately. It had all the marks of a deliberate insult.

I want to maintain that the universe is in many ways like that. All analogies need to be handled with care. They cannot prove anything and always assume the thing they try to illustrate. But my argument will be that the universe as a whole, and certain aspects of it in particular, leave us with a very strong impression that they are the work of a personal Creator. Indeed we are made aware that he is there.

The analogy of the Hyde Park orator is useful in one important respect. The speaker made an inference from a purely mechanical event (tomato in the air) to something of a totally different kind: some*one* hostile to him. He was not asking what kind of physical force had projected the tomato. He thought he knew that. He was asking 'Who?' because he wanted to confront the culprit. There was no suggestion that the event defied the normal expectations of physics and chemistry. But it seemed to the speaker to have a significance in the realm of ideas and relationships between people. It had aspects which made it a different kind of event from a purely mechanical happening.

The logic of the Christian position

There are at least two ways of tackling a question of this kind and they involve two kinds of mental process – what could be called two kinds of logic. The traditional Christian method, and the method of most philosophy, has been to establish certain agreed starting points (*e.g.* that there is no effect without a cause), and then to argue from that in accordance with traditional logic, *i.e.* in the same sort of way that we usually argue in mathematics. The criticisms of this sort of reasoning are rightly concerned, firstly with the validity of the starting points, and secondly with whether the case follows absolutely logically from the starting points. Today the classical 'proofs' for the existence of God seem weak to most people on the first count: the starting points assume too much. But they do have a further great weakness as well. The highly abstract kind of starting point and the severely mathematical kind of subsequent argument can lead only to highly abstract conclusions. Such a method might, if successful, demonstrate an 'uncaused cause' for instance. But an uncaused cause is a very distorted description of God and is hardly an object of love and worship.

Mercifully a great deal of our thinking does not follow this kind of mathematical model. We do most of our day-to-day reasoning by a method which is much more like the diagnosis of a disease, the identification of a make of car, the reading of complex sentences of print, or the recognition of a family likeness. To take the last example: no doubt family features can be analysed fairly precisely. If we tried we should end up with a whole series of variables within certain limits. But when we meet a girl and immediately recognize the child of her mother, for instance, we would often find it impossible to analyse the factors. Some are physical, some are matters of expression and manner. But at times the recognition is absolutely convincing. There *is* the likeness. It has, of course, a physical basis; but it is more than the sum of its parts. It is a different *kind* of thing from saying that the nose has certain measurements. We have recognized a personal relationship and we are not wrong. If we stop to discuss the details we lose the point; and yet the picture as a whole does consist of details and relationships between details. There is no either/or between the detailed measurements that could be made and the blood relationship. There may not be time or opportunity to check our recognition, but if there is and we can ask the girl what her name is, and her mother's name, then we will be doubly sure.

The arguments that I want to bring forward to show that there is a Creator God are of this second kind. They may not of themselves each one be conclusive, but fitted together they create a picture which is to many people convincing. They are not mathematical proofs and if treated as such they are confusing. There is no QED to put at the end of the discussion. What the Christian ends up by saying is: 'Can't you see, then, that there is God?' He is saying more than that God is the best hypothesis to account for these phenomena and that he is therefore probable. The Christian is saying that he himself sees the likeness as something positive and unavoidable. He is compelled to think in terms of personal activity behind the world. He can trace out some of its features. He must therefore ask the doubter to do the same and to see if it doesn't become a convincing picture of a personal God.

This kind of thinking, which is more typical of history and biological sciences than mathematics or philosophy, is every bit as reasonable as traditional philosophical thinking and it is by no means always less certain in its results. In many areas deductive thinking simply cannot help us much. In fact, of course, most disciplines provide a mixture of these two kinds of logic and perhaps others as well.[1] But there are several features of this 'recognition of a picture' kind of thinking that are worth mentioning. We recognize a reality *of a different kind* from the bare elements of which it is made up (*e.g.* a blood relationship is seen by the shape of the face). Such recognition depends on seeing the picture *as a whole*: it is often also an *all-or-none* affair and therefore it is often *sudden*. After puzzling for some time over the meaning of a sentence or a poem, or the solution of a political problem, we suddenly 'see' the answer. Even in science, which is usually thought of as primarily mathematical, discoveries have quite often been more of this kind than the end point of a long and complex calculation. Kékulé, who had for a long time puzzled over the nature of the benzene molecule, suddenly thought of a *ring* of six carbon atoms and immediately recognized it as almost certainly the answer. Archimedes is supposed to have discovered his principle one day in his bath and to have dashed out into the street naked and shouting 'Eureka' (I have found it). The human mind often works by trying out the possible 'fit' of a series of co-ordinating ideas to a set of facts. Sometimes none of them will do; then suddenly a new one provides an answer. It needs to be followed through with checks in matters of detail, but the initial discovery may come in an overall picture or 'Gestalt' that is immediately convincing. The logic of faith is quite frequently like that and the task of the Christian, therefore, as much as anything else, is to show how the facts fit together to provide a pattern or picture that speaks to us of a personal God rather than a mere First Cause or Ideal.

Most of the ordinary decisions of life are reasonable but based on this kind of reasoning. Our relationships to our friends are based on our view of them as a whole. Our political and social and artistic tastes are based on wide-ranging criticism and appreciation which we can only par-

[1] The textbooks of logic discuss inductive and deductive reasoning but do not always give sufficient thought to what could be called 'conceptual' or 'Gestalt' reasoning which is what I am concerned with here.

tially break down into detailed arguments. The kind of certainty we arrive at by such thinking is often not so clear cut as in mathematics and physics, but it can be nonetheless strong enough to control most of the really important things in life – choosing a training, choosing a job, deciding our obligations and priorities in life, marriage, friends, how we spend our time and money.

Take another example. In a murder mystery, before the murderer can be named, twelve impartial jury men have to be convinced that he is guilty. They have both to eliminate the obvious alternatives, including accidental death, and also to reconstruct the picture so that it makes convincing sense *as a whole*. No particular piece of evidence is in itself conclusive, unless it is in the sense of being just the last point which correlates an otherwise baffling collection of apparently unconnected facts. But the conviction comes from facing the picture as a whole. Some points are essential to the case and if they were proved false the whole case would collapse. Much depends on the clarity and conviction with which these cardinal factors are demonstrated. But even so, if we concentrate entirely on these particular items piecemeal, we shall never come to a conclusion. We have got to be willing to stand back from the detail and try to see it whole.

Is it proved?

If it is asked whether it can be proved that there is a Creator God the answer must be 'No'. In the ordinary, strict sense of the word 'prove' it cannot be done. But in that sense of the word very few important things can be proved. We cannot even prove our own existence, or the existence of a world outside our own minds, and yet we do not doubt these things.

So, although God cannot be proved, that does not mean that the discussion is a waste of time. On the contrary I want to try to show in this section that the evidence that there is a personal Creator is such that we cannot ignore it. Some have argued that the whole discussion can serve only to give a bit more content to the name 'God' for the benefit of those who already believe in him. Although it will do that, of course, I believe it does much more. It helps, for example, to show that the Christian idea of a Creator God makes very good sense. Negatively it helps to show that it is not unreasonable to believe. Positively it helps to show that the Christian view is as good as any, and probably very much better because it corresponds better to the facts. There is a definite push towards faith. The result is that we are left under an obligation to pursue the subject further and to see what other kinds of evidence there may be. If Christianity seriously might be true it is very important indeed. We cannot brush the question aside. I want to show that there is at least enough in the evidence for a Creator to leave us blameworthy if we do not follow it up. Indeed the discussion is intended to show us that we are confronted by God in his creation.

At this point people sometimes object that five weak arguments do not make one strong one. That is perfectly true if we are thinking of 'proofs' in the mathematical sense. But five pieces of a jig-saw puzzle, each of which contains only strong hints of its meaning, may add up to an undoubted picture of a face or a house or a ship, *etc.* One of our troubles today is that we are so specialized; we are scientists, or artists, or historians or social workers. For many of the most important purposes in life we have to get out of our narrow speciality and try to be straightforward human beings again, looking at life as a whole. Added together and related to one another I believe that these evidences confront us with a personal Creator – we become aware that he is there all the time. We must therefore go on to look at five points which I believe are most compelling pointers to God the Creator. I have called them: the fact of existence, the nature of the universe, the meaning of human life, the moral universe and the innate sense of God. They are all capable of much more detailed analysis but I believe they are best discussed briefly and bluntly so that we do not get lost in the detail.

Many people, of course, have come to a firm belief in a

Creator God from such evidence. This has often been true even when they could in no sense be called Christian, and this is often still true today. To very large numbers of people of all cultures the existence of a Creator is pretty 'obvious'. They look at the natural order and draw this conclusion without any difficulty. This is the chief basis of the similarities between some of the great religions which it is now so popular to stress. Many, but not all, of the world's religions acknowledge an all-powerful Creator. He may, or may not, be important in the system of beliefs, but they usually regard it as clear that such a being exists.[2] I want next to examine the grounds for such belief. If we cleared our minds of all superstition and tradition, what reasons would remain for such belief? I believe that there is a wide range of evidence that is valid and important and I want to select what seem to be the most cogent points for discussion, even though the ground covered is admittedly selective.

[2] From this point on, of course, the religions diverge. Some ignore the Creator and concern themselves with lesser forces of good or evil. Some concentrate on ethical or philosophical teaching. Some more or less identify the Creator with the universe he has created, and there are plenty of other alternatives. Christianity alone knows that the personal Creator has personally entered his own world in order to deal with man's sin and so make a living relationship with God a daily reality.

2. The fact of the universe

There are two distinct points that need to be made under this heading and it is important not to confuse them. The first is the fact of existence – the fact, that is, that there is anything at all to talk about when we consider the world, other people and our own physical life. How does it come about that people and things exist at all? The second question is concerned with the *kind* of universe we live in. Does the nature of the world tell us anything about its meaning and origin? These are the points to which two of the traditional 'five ways' or 'proofs' attempted an answer (the cosmological and teleological arguments). Our approach is different from these 'proofs', but the questions they tried to deal with remain valid.

The fact of existence

First, we have to stop and stand back from the universe to ask, how do we explain it? I say we *have* to ask. It would be more correct to say that it is 'natural' to ask, because it is hard to believe that the universe is self-explanatory. The answer could be that the universe just is. The non-Christian can argue like this: 'The tomato-thrower was not unique. When the speaker saw the tomato he knew that events *like that* usually have a human agent. But there is by definition only one universe and we cannot compare the universe with its parts without further discussion. It is possible to maintain that, whereas everything within the universe is explained by reference to other things within the universe, the universe as a whole is simply self-explanatory.' The trouble is that to almost everybody it is not self-explanatory. If nothing else in life is self-explanatory we feel it is not quite honest to avoid the problem by saying that this is the one exception, especially since we are talking about a physical system — the material universe. We feel that there is enough analogy to events within the world for us to have to ask: what or who is its explanation?

There seem to be three kinds of answer to this question. First, some people adopt an agnostic position and say they do not know and do not see how they can know. This book is an attempt to respond to that kind of agnosticism. There are a very few dogmatic agnostics who assert that we cannot possibly know, but such dogmatic agnosticism is very hard to justify. How can one so confidently know that we cannot know? Most agnostics remain open to persuasion and willing to think again. Their agnosticism is an interim and not necessarily a final position.

Secondly, there are those who propose various kinds of process as the answer to the question. Some talk in terms of 'Evolution' or 'Continuous creation', or 'cyclical processes', or just 'Nature', or other more detailed processes which we can observe on a small scale. The Christian is bound to say that, however much truth there may be in these marvellous processes, they do not really answer the problem. Evolution (however big the capital E with which it is spelt), or Nature, or any of the other processes are not, in principle, more than an explanation of what is going on within the universe. They do not tell us how it comes to be that there is a universe at all. In principle (not necessarily in detail) they might all be correct and there might still be a personal Creator. We would still be left asking how it comes to be that there is a 'Nature', or that 'Evolution' has taken place. Some writers, whose thinking is not in my view Christian, give the name God to one or other of these processes. But that is to degrade the idea of God; these are only processes we observe within the universe.

Thirdly, Christians, and many others, say that the only

satisfactory answer is that there is a personal Creator who made it all. How he made it is irrelevant here. They affirm that the universe cries out for that kind of an explanation. Our mind cannot rest until it thinks in such terms. It seems to most people 'natural', even 'obvious', that the incredible world we live in is the result of the action of a great and wonderful, personal Creator.

If this is the 'natural' explanation for most people we must recognize, however, that the 'natural' explanation is not always the right one, and in this case there is a further problem. If God created the universe is he 'self-explanatory' or do we 'naturally' go on to ask for an explanation of God? The answer, I believe, is that most people are able to accept the idea of God as self-explanatory even when they cannot do the same for the universe. For one thing God is outside time, which he created, whereas the universe and the whole idea of cause and effect are concepts dependent on time. God is a different kind of reality from the universe and to ask about God's existence turns out to be a different kind of question from asking about that of the universe. There is an analogy with the tomato-thrower here. Such an event asks for explanation in personal terms and our minds can rest when we know that John Smith threw it. To go on and ask about John Smith and his motives is a different kind of question and raises different kinds of problems from the problem of 'Who threw it?' For most purposes our mind is able to rest when it has settled that primary question. The further question may be asked, but for our present purpose the point is that the universe looks like the product of a personal Creator. In fact we are at times aware of him through the world that he has made. If we were trying to prove an 'uncaused cause' we would certainly have to go on to answer questions about the 'origin' of God. But we are simply saying that the universe leads us to believe that there is a Creator. It asks for that kind of explanation.

The vast majority of people of almost all ages and cultures have in fact agreed that the universe does imply a Creator. Just how he is envisaged varies considerably but he is nearly always thought of as personal, or at least not less than personal. There are two reasons for that. First, the only creative agencies we know of are personal. Less than personal agencies do not show real creative ability in the same sense, though they may perform remarkable feats of instinctive and relatively rigidly predictable construction, such as nest building. When we say that the universe needs to be explained in terms of a Creator we mean a Creator who has at least the kind of unique creative abilities that persons have, and very much more. Secondly, it is usually accepted that the Creator cannot be less in quality than his creation and the highest thing we know of in the universe is personality. All talk of a Creator, in the sense in which we have been discussing it, is therefore almost taken for granted to be talk of a Power of not less than personal qualities. No doubt he is far greater than our concept of personality, but what exactly greater than personal qualities might be is hard for us to say. We have no words or images to describe such a reality unless we go on to talk about the self-revelation of God. For this stage in the discussion, therefore, it is enough to say that the very fact that the universe exists and confronts us is enough to evoke in us the idea of a personal God and a strong suspicion that he is there.

As a rule this strikes us most strongly not when we are in need or crisis, but when we are faced with some particularly good experience. Human love, the birth of a child, an experience of unusual beauty in nature, for example, seem to bring us face to face most forcibly with this sense of being in a universe made by God. It is not that these things have no 'scientific explanation'. We may know all about the processes that are involved. It is certainly not that they are scientifically queer. The fact is that they make us aware of something of a different order. They have a language that cannot be expressed in terms of their machinery and we read in them features of a kind totally different from the understanding we may have of how they have come about. 'The heavens', says the psalmist, 'are telling the glory of God . . . Day to day pours forth speech, and night to night declares knowledge. There is no speech, nor are there words; their voice is not heard; yet their voice goes out through all the earth, and their words to the end of the world.'[1] That is to say there is nothing that *compels* belief. There may be no explicit demonstrations of God, no 'miraculous' features which declare God's presence, no audible or visible words. Yet there is a message. Often we read the message unwillingly, but it stares us in the face.

What kind of a universe is it?

The nineteenth-century apologists found what they thought were unanswerable arguments for God in the details of the design of the world. Water, for instance, is most dense at 4° C just before it freezes. One consequence is that the water in ponds and rivers and the sea mixes until it cools down to 4° C and then, if the temperature cools further, freezes from the top downwards and not from the bottom upwards. As a result life is possible in large areas of water which would otherwise freeze solid. Again, the earth, unless it is much over-cultivated, produces a continuous series of harvests so that, until he overpopulates an area, man is able to live and enjoy adequate food year after year. These writers also found exciting evidence in the detailed design of the human body, for example the hand and eye. Pointing to their superb adaptation to their function they asked how we could possibly explain these details without postulating a Creator.

In its old form this argument is not really logically compelling to most people today. We now have alternative 'explanations' for the adaptation of living things to their environment and the universe is so large and varied that we are told that by the mere laws of chance all kinds of conditions suitable to life must occur somewhere. If they occur on this planet they will almost certainly be present on others of the millions of planets we now believe exist.

We could grant all these theories and yet the argument from the appearance of design would not altogether die. The reason is that, when all has been said on the other side, we are still filled with astonishment when we understand

[1] Psalm 19 : 1, 2.

even a small part of the intricacies and harmonies of nature. If births, and life-long marriages, and good health, and our ability to enjoy the beauty of colour and sound in nature were not commonplace we might well deny that they were possible. It is doubtful if anyone would believe the processes of mammalian birth if it didn't happen so often! The world is almost incredible in detail as well as in the overall fact of its existence. The more we know about science the easier it is in many ways to be moved to awe. Trees are beautiful, but to have some understanding of how they work leaves us full of admiration and wonder. At such a point we have to ask ourselves: at whom or at what am I marvelling? The fact is that the universe has an almost incredible unity and apparent plan. It is a 'universe' and not a 'multiverse'! It is infinitely ingenious. Its unity is such that man's most advanced scientific and technological interventions are liable to be nearly disastrous in their effects. The balance and harmony of nature is so vastly superior to the best that man can do. We are simply reduced to silence when we face it and all our scientific knowledge is as nothing.

It is true, of course, that all the intricate adaptations of living things to their environment have one kind of explanation in terms of evolutionary theory. If animals and plants were not well adapted they would not survive. Natural selection, it is said, has eliminated (or is eliminating) what was poorly adapted and has been the means of ensuring that the better adaptations have survived. This is not the place to go into the technical debate about the question. But even if all the claims of the most extreme evolutionist were accepted, he is proposing simply a mechanism whereby such adaptations have been brought into being. The mechanism itself, if it has such possibilities, cannot but astonish us. If the original built-in possibilities of matter are such that *living* matter can exist in such varieties and with such perfect adaptations, we have just as much cause for standing back in awe and wonder at the whole complex web of the universe as if it had appeared suddenly from nothing in an obviously miraculous way. It is not that any particular thing in the natural order is scientifically impossible. Presumably it all has a scientific basis, even when we don't yet know what it is. But it is so marvellously fitted together.

The argument is not that in the details we can see that the thing 'could not have happened' without God. It is rather that the universe is in its details the *kind of* universe that asks for an explanation in terms of a personal Creator. It is so incredibly complex and so marvellously integrated, the capacity for adaptation of living things to the physical world is so great, that most people are moved to wonder and awe and are gradually forced to say that the universe has qualities that we most naturally explain in terms of a very great mind behind it.

It can be replied that we ought to have our capacity for understanding things in purely physico-chemical terms expanded! There are some very marvellous things that we can see are 'just' the result of physico-chemical forces – the pattern in snowflakes for instance. Indeed I am not trying to argue that at the scientific level it is not *all* just the result of scientific forces. My point is that it makes us also ask questions of a non-scientific kind. Could all this have come about without a mind of almost incredible wisdom behind it? Is it the kind of thing – snowflakes and all – which we can really dismiss in purely impersonal terms? Even if we understood it all scientifically should we not, just as much as if we could not understand, be so filled with wonder at it that we should want to attribute it to an all-wise Creator?

The universe in fact is the *kind* of thing that needs to be explained in terms of mind as well as process. There are plenty of things in life which require explanation on several levels. To take a very ordinary example, a car is a piece of machinery whose production follows altogether scientific laws. But it is also, perhaps, a symbol of Japanese trade or the brain-child of Henry Ford. Or to take another example: if in exploring a cave we find scratches on the wall we shall ask not only whether these scratches were made by wood, stone or metal. We shall also ask a higher level question. Were they made by animate or inanimate forces? If the former, were they made by men or animals? If by men, are they meant to convey a message or not? We shall constantly be 'stepping up' the question as we proceed, even when we have given an exhaustive answer to the previous question. The man who believes these marks are primitive art or writing has to show us that this is so, not by proving the incompleteness of lower level answers but by showing us the internal consistency and convincing nature of the explanation at the higher levels of significance that he claims is there. For instance he must show that it really does make sense as writing. That description is complementary to, and not contradictory to, the description of it as marks made by a flint or other very hard stone.

It is possible of course to claim that the whole world simply does not seem to require any explanation except in terms of science. But is that honestly convincing? The Christian says that he sees in the creation some aspects of God's work; 'The invisible things of him (God) . . . are clearly seen, being understood by the things that are made' (Rom. 1: 20, AV). We shall not get nearer or further from it by discussing science. People must be asked to look at the natural world in a different way and invited to ask the sort of question that human beings must ask – at least sometimes. What at this kind of level does it all signify? Can I honestly dismiss it as less than the creation and plan of a mighty personal God? Like seeing a face hidden in a picture-puzzle of trees and stones and clouds, do we not at least sometimes see 'a face' so clearly that we have to acknowledge that it really is there and that the picture is not understood until we admit that that is what it is really about?

3. Does science explain it all away?

One major reply to the argument thus far will undoubtedly have come to mind. There are plenty of people who say that, whatever the indications may be of a God responsible for the universe, they are all explained away by science. The argument as most commonly developed has two prongs.

First, the fact that looking at nature turns us almost instinctively to belief in God is said to be due to our psychological history which leaves most of us needing some psychological prop of this kind. God is either a Father-figure substitute or some other form of invention of our sub-conscious designed to satisfy certain psychological needs.

Second, it is argued that logically no such hypothesis as God is in fact necessary. Everything that man has studied so far is increasingly explicable in terms of physics and chemistry. There is no reason to think that there is any exception to this rule. The frontiers of scientific knowledge move inexorably forward. Numerous strong points at which Christians postulated the necessary activity of God and the improbability of any adequate scientific explanation have already been overrun. Christians postulated God's direct action in so many positions where they have been proved wrong that we have every reason to believe that they are wrong altogether. The world shows every sign of being nothing but a system of impersonal cause and effect which, when it gets complex enough, produces self-consciousness and the other higher aspects of humanity, but in the final analysis is no more than matter in motion. The idea of God was a childlike mistake produced in order to fill the gaps in our knowledge because we were not mature enough to face the harsh realities of our situation.

Psychological explanations of faith

The psychological argument has the great weakness that it is entirely two-edged. If belief in God is produced by the sub-conscious desire for a Father-figure, then disbelief in God can equally be produced by a sub-conscious desire to reinforce our independence of any kind of Father-figure. Arguing that way we can conclude only that beliefs have little to do with truth and that atheism and theism alike leave the question entirely open. There still may be a God even if our reasons for believing in him are bad ones; and atheism could still be true even if all atheists were merely satisfying a desire for psychological independence of their parents. Atheism might be psychologically more attractive to independent people striving to be adult but, nevertheless, totally mistaken.

The discussion of psychological motives really gets us nowhere. Take politics as an example. The fact that many people vote for their party for irrelevant psychological reasons does not settle the question as to whether one party's policy really is calculated to serve the interest of the community better than the other. It is relevant to warn people that their political beliefs may be purely selfish, or traditional, but having done that we must go on to argue a *rational* case for our party. If we believe that all political views are really irrational the only thing to do is to stop arguing and start brainwashing, or manipulating the electorate in some other way.

It is the same in matters of faith. The response to our knowledge of how beliefs and unbeliefs are formed is either to acknowledge the need to be self-critical and then to continue the argument as rationally as possible or, alternatively, to take up a position not of atheism nor even of agnosticism but of complete cynicism about all beliefs including our own belief in cynicism. If this argument invalidates faith it invalidates lack of faith and every other position as well.

'Nothing but'

The same is even more true of the second prong of the argument – that all reality is *nothing but* matter in motion. In its strong form it invalidates all thought. Not many people would want to hold it in that form, but if reality is nothing but matter in motion, then my thoughts are nothing but physical events in my brain. That surely implies that thoughts can tell me nothing reliable about reality. My physical senses, such as sight, tell me about what I think is physical reality in a way that is effective and useful, and the different senses give me a consistent picture of the physical aspects of reality. But how can a mere collection of electronic recording systems linked to a corresponding motor system have any reliable ideas about itself or about reality as a whole? If that is all it is, the 'feeling' that no other sort of reality exists or the 'feeling' that it does exist are equally just irrational by-products of the state of electrons in the central nervous system. On that view all discussion and thought about the meaning of life is futile because all argument is merely the statement of how at this particular moment I itch. This conclusion is self-defeating.

But it is also unbelievable. We cannot avoid the conviction that we do know something about reality in the same way that we cannot avoid the conclusion that we exist. It is intellectually possible to doubt both for short periods, but it is not possible to live with, or to act on, these doubts. We would not even be justified in committing suicide; we should want to rid ourselves of the illusion and sleep forever with indefinite sweet dreams. But we keep on waking up to find both ourselves and a reality outside ourselves. Drugs, which are popular partly because they appear to offer such an escape, prove very transitory and leave the user with a severe hangover even when they are not in the long run lethal. We come back to the conviction that we do know something

36

about reality and that it is worth arguing about it and moulding it for our own good and the good of others. We cannot postulate that it is nothing but matter in motion and at the same time say that our belief that that is true has any meaning at all.[1]

Most people, therefore, feel after some weaker form of this argument. Some say that the only thing *we can be sure of* is that there is matter in motion. That fact we know and for the rest it is an open question. But the fact that we are sure of this metaphysical truth itself implies that there is more to reality than matter in motion. It implies that such a thing as metaphysical truth can be known even in a purely negative form. It is very hard to see how anyone can have it both ways. If once you allow that we can know that kind of statement about reality to be true, then we ought at least to be open to discover other similar truths – truths which are not in themselves mere equations in terms of physics and chemistry but have a reality of another kind. It does not seem possible to find a way between a strong position which is self-defeating and one which leaves everything open and cannot deny the Christian position *if* that position is supported by good evidence.[2]

[1] The logical result of this sort of view of life may seem to be to try to 'drop out' into some form of mysticism which treats all reality as illusion, and tries to find release by meditating on the 'beyond' or in an unreal experience induced by drugs. In this sense some people do *try* to make a way of life out of this philosophy and almost persuade themselves that it is true, until they are brought down to earth again with a bump by the need to acquire the physical necessities of life or by discovering something of the marvellous range of experience that God has for us in the real world – such as falling in love with a genuine flesh-and-blood person. They then have to face reality again. The inexperienced may despise such a person as having destroyed their vision. But in fact it is experience that has cured them of an illusion. It is experience of the real world that pushes us on towards faith.

[2] Even the logical positivists are in difficulties here. In laying down their verification principle (see A. J. Ayer, *Language, Truth & Logic*, Gollancz, 1936) they have started with a principle that cannot itself be verified. If their principle is valid then they must allow that others may propound other principles of like kind and believe them equally reasonably. The very fact that they have such a principle opens the door to beliefs that that particular principle denies.

The stop-gap God

No-one has yet got round this dilemma; but supposing that they could, what of the main part of this second prong of the attack? The argument is that everything we know about has a scientific basis – in terms of matter-in-motion – and that that is all it is. If we can satisfactorily explain it in these terms why introduce any others? God was usually just a stop-gap for our ignorance. Whenever we fill the gaps God is excluded.

Let us take the example of the mechanical understanding of the solar system. Isaac Newton's superb system 'explained' almost all the phenomena in mechanical and mathematical terms. But he still invoked God both as 'the very First Cause, which certainly is not mechanical . . .', and also as one 'Who being in all Places, is more able by His will to move the bodies with His boundless sensorium, and thereby to form and *reform* the parts of the universe . . . ' (our italics).[3] That is to say, he invoked God as a First Cause and also brought him in to correct by direct interposition those ir-regularities which may gradually accumulate in the solar system. Laplace showed that this latter point was not neces-sary and that these irregularities in fact corrected them-selves. When Laplace went to present his book to Napoleon, the Emperor asked how it was that he had not even men-tioned the Creator. To this he replied, 'I have no need of that hypothesis.' He did not deny God as a Creator, but he denied the necessity of God as a physical force within his world. The point has often been máde that if the Newtonians found evidence *for* God in their partial understanding of natural laws, then the fact that God proved unnecessary to understanding the processes of the universe was at least a further weakening of the arguments for God. Laplace him-self did not draw this conclusion, but many others have done so, and if it were true that the evidence for God depended on showing that God acts as a physical force in the material world, then the case would be extremely weak – indeed disastrously so.

[3] I. Newton, *Opticks*, 3rd ed., Query 28 and pp. 379 and 378. Quoted by W. C. Dampier in *A History of Science*, 3rd ed., 1942, p. 188.

Newton was not at all a good theologian, however, although he was probably the world's greatest mathematician. He was one of the founders of the tradition which first regarded nature as a machine and then, to allow for the apparently non-mechanical aspects, allowed both God and man (and, perhaps, angels and devils) to 'intervene' and alter the 'set' of the machine. This has been called the 'God of the gaps' argument and it must be admitted that it was mistaken because the activity of God in nature is not to be seen as that of a machine repairer. According to the Bible we see God in nature in the regularities – the things that we do understand scientifically – even more than in the things that we don't understand. He is its originator and he keeps it in being. It declares his glory by what it is. The relationship between our scientific knowledge of the world and our theological knowledge of the world is the relationship between two dimensions of description, or two levels, and not two departments of knowledge in the same plane.

People have developed this point in different ways for a long time. It was in fact being urged by Christian writers at least 100 years ago,[4] but it is common for non-Christian writers to hark back to the God-of-the-gaps argument even today as if it was the only Christian view of the matter. Karl Heim in the 1920s talked about different 'spaces'. Even if we describe the world as a machine it has been pointed out that a machine is something other than the sum of its parts.[5] It is not more than the sum of its parts in the sense that there are pieces of metal that appear from nowhere when it is put together. It is more, however, in the sense that, when seen as a whole, it has quite another kind of significance. As every

[4] See, e.g., Archbishop Trench in his book *Notes on the Miracles of our Lord*, 1866 (Pickering and Inglis, 1958).

[5] *E.g.* by Professor Michael Polanyi. This is important because the idea of nature as a machine has been extremely fruitful in science. It has its limitations, but is often claimed to be the basis of much scientific advance and to be in itself some sort of denial of God. Polanyi shows that at least this claim to exclude God does not follow at all. See 'Life Transcending Physics and Chemistry' in *Chemical and Engineering News* (August 21, 1967); 'On the Modern Mind' in *Encounter* (May, 1965); 'Life's Irreducible Structure' in *Science* (Vol. 160, June 21, 1968).

child knows, when bricks are put together to make a garage or a house there comes a point where we say, not 'There are so many bricks arranged in the following pattern', but 'There is a garage'. It is defined not in terms of its parts but in terms of its function. The two descriptions are quite different and as far as each is concerned the other does not matter greatly. As far as the function is concerned it matters very little what the building units are. As far as a brick-maker is concerned it matters very little what they will be used to build.

If nature is correctly thought of as a machine, then that in itself means that we allow that it has significance outside itself. Indeed all machines have to be defined in terms outside themselves if we are to describe their function, or if not their function at least their boundaries. A machine is a collection of parts combined in a certain way *so that* it will do particular things. We may define and analyse all the parts of an aeroplane and their relationships to one another, but if we do not mention that it is a flying machine we shall fail to understand it. The concept of flight is not implied by any of its detailed parts. A friend of the author who was learning to fly confessed that he was far too frightened to leave the ground but enjoyed running the machine around as if it were a fast car! But it is not a good car because it is built to fly. Our understanding of the parts of any machine and their relationships in terms of physics and chemistry and mechanics could be 100 per cent complete and still not tell us the most important thing we want to know. The two kinds of description are totally different, but if we call it a machine we imply that both kinds of description are possible.

Levels of reality

That is where the phrase 'nothing but' confuses the issue. What has been called 'nothing buttery' consists of the simple error of saying that the aeroplane is nothing but metal. Even if it were true from one point of view it would be untrue as soon as we ask what kind of a thing the machine as a whole is.

This approach can be developed in several ways.[6] In the physical world we are at times faced with the fact that the useful descriptions of a phenomenon are in such different frames of reference that, even though they may at first glance appear to contradict one another, they are in fact complementary, in the same sort of way that plan and elevation drawings of a building are complementary, though at first they appear to be drawings of two different things. The classical example in physics is the relation between the wave and corpuscular theories of light.

Take for instance a human being as an example. We can talk chemistry about him. Indeed we can talk inorganic chemistry. From one point of view he is *only* so much carbon, hydrogen, oxygen, nitrogen, phosphorus, sulphur, *etc.* There are no mysterious elements that we need to add to make up a living organism. But to say that the difference between two animals is the percentage of phosphorus in their composition may be true at the level of the chemist's catalogue, but is almost totally unhelpful to the biologist. It is more useful to talk bio-chemistry and to say that the elements are combined in certain ways and that the compounds have certain properties. Even so we have no terms even for 'life' and 'death' in the bio-chemical equations, let alone terms for species, adaptations, ecological habits, *etc.* The Dalmatian is probably unique amongst dogs in his nitrogen excretion but that is not the best way to identify him.

Even if the bio-chemical description were complete the biologist would want to come along and add a whole group of scientific ideas and categories that are simply not bio-chemistry and cannot in principle be described in chemical formulae. To say that this specimen is an adult male of moderate intelligence and manual dexterity tells us a lot of things that no doubt have a bio-chemical basis, at least in

[6] Prof. D. M. MacKay's *The Clockwork Image* (IVP, 1974) is a good example. Many non-Christians agree, of course, that 'reductionism' is an error and that we are wrong to try to reduce the world to its scientific processes.

the genetic code, but are not that kind of thing at all. Maleness and femaleness are not the differences between two chemical compounds, they are biological differences whose meaning needs to be defined in terms of psychology, physiology, and reproductive rôle, *etc.* We do not need to know any bio-chemistry in order to be able to talk significantly and usefully about the differences between the sexes. When the biologist has said all he wants to say, however, there is more. The psychologist, sociologist, the economist and the anthropologist, each want to have their slice and each claim to talk meaningfully and usefully about man with very little reference to biology. And so one could go on. The point is that for such a complex thing as man there is a hierarchy of levels. In each, in theory at least, one could give a complete description of man and leave nothing out, in the same way as a plan drawing leaves out nothing in that plane. The question is, What other planes or levels should be described for other purposes?

What the Christian is claiming about the world is not that at the physico-chemical level there are gaps that we must attribute to God's activity. On the contrary, when a complete description has been given at that level we can start again and give complementary (and in principle complete) descriptions in different terms at several other levels. The most comprehensive level, the Christian says, needs to be in terms of God and his relationships to his world. If we omit that level we do not do justice to the reality that it is. We teach children to read by studying ink marks on paper. At first they may call it scribble and see no real difference between one kind of scribble and another. Then they learn, not that letters are written in a different kind of ink, but that mere ink marks on paper (which is all it is at that level) can also talk to us. We ask, 'What does it say?' The difference between a page of words talking sense and one talking nonsense may be negligibly small (the alteration of the order of two letters for instance), but it is an absolute difference on another level. One says something; the other says nothing.

The Christian, then, is basically asking whether, when we look at the world, it doesn't say something about God. Perhaps it is not very clear always, but he asserts that he sees the activity of God and cannot honestly explain it away in lower level categories. In the last resort he is trying to teach his friends to 'read' nature in a new way. This need not involve any scientific knowledge, but it is perfectly compatible with all the scientific explanations in the world and all that we shall ever have in the future. The more or less completeness of the scientific world picture is not relevant. Supposing it was 100 per cent complete we should still need to stand back and ask, 'Does the universe not speak of a Creator and a Creator who in his power and wisdom has created a unity?'

There is no more reason to say that it is all 'nothing but' scientific cause and effect than to say that it is all nothing but economics. Why should science describe the limits of our knowledge? Is it not quite clear that other kinds of description may be equally valid and equally useful? But each description of course has to be convincing on its own level, otherwise we would be in danger of accepting nonsense.

The swing from science

We are in fact today confronted with an interesting reaction against science and technology. It is not only the reaction to the atom bomb and environmental pollution that has caused this. These are extreme examples of the situation as a whole. We realize clearly how much more important decisions of another kind often are. Indeed we know well that it is on other levels than the scientific that the most important discoveries and decisions are made. Environmental problems involve questions of what we should value in life. The atom bomb problem really takes us straight back to the kindergarten: who is going to hit first and will they dare to in view of the likely retaliation? Sometimes it looks like the problem of who is going to lose his temper first. More and more people are criticizing science and scientists for being unable to grapple with the 'real' problem and they are turning to arts subjects in the hope of finding solutions there. The swing from science and the reaction from scientism are signs of the same realization of the limitation of science. Because some of the advocates of science have claimed too much many people now reject science as a dangerous over-simplification.

There are in fact signs that this reaction is going too far and Christians are now frequently found amongst those who are defending science and technology, defending them, that is, not as the solution of all problems but as good and worth-while activities *within their own scope.* The Christian is equally unable to share the enthusiasm of those who think that the cure for all our ills is in politics. The solution of our problem does not lie in any of these directions. We need science and we need politics and 'arts and inventions and daring enterprises'. But unless they are seen in their true perspective they are bound to produce disillusionment when we discover how limited their scope is. They are excellent in as far as they go, but they cover only one aspect or relatively limited level of reality. Whether or not other levels, including a comprehensive Christian level, are valid cannot be settled by the appeal to science as an alternative.

4. The problem of evil

This is not the place to present a full discussion of the problem of evil, but in its various forms it remains probably the chief objection to the position adopted in this book and is for many people the major obstacle to any kind of belief in God. It is argued that, if God is a real God – the almighty Creator – then evil seems to show that he is not altogether good. If, on the other hand, it is insisted that he is good, then how does it come about that he co-exists with evil unless he is not, after all, almighty? In particular, the positive view of the natural world as evidence for God that this book has argued invites a come-back. If Christians appeal to the universe and say that it 'tells the glory of God', how do they explain the presence of evil? Does that also tell the glory of a God who allows it to go on? The non-Christian has a right to suggest that the problem is one particularly acute for the Christian. If he hadn't appealed to nature his dilemma would be less. Even those who do not believe in a personal Creator have a real, though different, problem of evil; but the Christian must show how evil co-exists with an all powerful and loving Creator.

The Christian view of the world

If it was being claimed that nature shows without doubt the moral excellencies of God the problem would need a further discussion. But this is not our position. We have argued that nature speaks to us of an almighty Creator but that the positive indications in nature that he is good, loving to men and morally perfect are partial and confused by the clear evidence that there is evil in the world. The witness of nature taken by itself is therefore ambiguous on this point. The goodness of God is not unmistakably clear in the creation. Christians do not believe that the world is in an ideal state. They admit that if we go to nature to try to infer the moral character of God we get an unclear picture.

This is one of the situations where the Christian must be allowed to explain his position from the 'inside' and show that it is a consistent whole. The Christian view is that the goodness of God is known chiefly from other sources. To some extent the material world has been warped by evil. The effects of this evil become more apparent as we consider the more personal aspects of the world. In man himself evil can become demonic, but evil is also present in less obvious ways in nature. Nature as a whole is like a superb piece of music played by an orchestra whose members from time to time simply ignore the conductor. It is still recognizable as a superb piece of music. The individual players are usually playing very well. But because they are out of time they are also often out of harmony. The result is the most fearful discords, and yet we can still recognize some of the marvellous quality of what was intended by the composer. It is a strange mixture of harmony and disharmony, beauty and ugliness. Even a cancer, for instance, seems to be a case of essential life processes of great complexity and beauty getting out of balance.

The Christian view of man

Similarly the Christian does not, as is sometimes supposed, take an entirely good or an entirely evil view of man. He sees him as a greater and more wonderful creature than does the Humanist, for instance. The Christian has in many ways the highest view of what man is – spiritually, morally, and physically. But he has also in other respects a lower view of man. He can and should admire the most wonderful of all things in the world, while at the same time he does not hesitate to say that man is spiritually and morally perverted ('fallen' is the word usually used), a tragic but noble ruin.

The Christian estimate of man is therefore in this respect similar to the Christian estimate of nature as a whole. Both are seen at the same time as astonishingly wonderful works of God and also as spoiled by evil. In the last hundred years Christians have tended to stress the fact of evil in human nature because the general trend in the West has been to play it down and speak as if the trouble with individuals and societies were only a relatively superficial matter of environment. Christians have had to stress Jesus' teaching that evil comes up from within and defiles us and our societies. The result is that some people think of the Christian view of man as entirely negative. That is incorrect,[1] and today, when people often think of man as a mere nothing, Christians are quite consistent in stressing that that is not the Christian view either. To the Christian, man is the most wonderful thing in a very wonderful creation. But he shows the presence of evil in more naked and brutal forms than the rest of the creation. He is both better and worse than nature.

When the hymn writer said:

> 'And every prospect pleases
> And only man is vile'

he was wrong on two points. Not everything in nature should please us. That would be sentimental and is the sort of religion that refuses to kill off sacred cows. Equally, although man can be vile, he is often still capable of deeds of great nobility. He also has marvellous capacities which even vile men can usually exercise effectively. On the Christian view the most notable and crucial evil in the

[1] There are other reasons for stressing the evil in man. When it comes to the question of how man can be forgiven and reconciled to God we have to say that he has no merit or worthiness at all. Men are *totally* alienated from God. God's mercy is *entirely* undeserved. But socially man is not as vicious as he could be. He is still capable of some social good even while he hates and repudiates God. If we are talking theology man is totally lost; if we are talking sociology he is a mixture of good and evil.

whole world is man's rebellion against God. As a result man's nature is warped and he is both at war with himself and with his fellow men. Because his life is ex-centric he inevitably creates friction with himself and with others. But the whole creation is also in a non-ideal state. We do not have to try to pretend that all is right with the world. We know that it is not, though we insist that, if you listen, you can still hear the music and not only the discords. If nature does seem to be in some respects 'red in tooth and claw', it is in other respects breathtakingly wonderful.

Why does God allow evil?

How, then, can the Christian explain this state of affairs? There is a threefold answer. First, evil is not God's invention. He is always contrary to it. In the very dramatic presentation of the problem in the book of Job the devil, the originator of all evil in the world, is presented as if he were a dog, or perhaps a lion, on a chain. He is allowed to do a certain amount of mischief but is always liable to be checked and prevented from doing what he wants by the restraining hand of his owner. This explains the fact that Christians can both hate evil and disease and at the same time accept it as in God's wisdom allowed to some extent for some good reason. It explains why the greatest stimulus to medicine and education has historically been Christianity, while at the same time the Christian can accept evil when it hits him personally, and avoid bitterness or any sense of despair. Christ, we are told, came to destroy the works of the devil, and the Christian should also set himself to fight evil in all its forms, even though he may have to accept it in some measure for himself – as Christ did also.

Although it may sound a cliché there is a difference between accepting evil as for some reason *allowed* by God for the present and accepting it as in any sense pleasing to God. The Christian cannot believe the latter, though many other religions appear to do so. God is always presented as implacably hostile to evil in every form, but he does not destroy it all immediately or man would be destroyed with it. Like some physical diseases it is allowed to run a limited course because the patient would be killed by too drastic a cure. Evil is now too integral to man, and to a lesser extent to nature, for a direct attack upon it to be other than destructive. But God hates it and will overcome it in the best possible way. That, however, will involve creating a totally new heaven and a new earth. For the present he allows this imperfect universe to continue.

Secondly, God himself is not indifferent to it. He has in fact taken its worst aspects upon himself. The Christian's God is the God who so loved the world that he gave his only Son to suffer and die so that men should be delivered from evil even in its personal and vicious form of sin. The Christian picture of God must be allowed to hang together in its true pattern. If we deny that Christ came to die for our sins then the problem of evil becomes much more intractable. But God is the God of the incarnation and the cross. He doesn't sit remote and indifferent on Olympus and allow his creatures to suffer without sharing it. He came into the world and experienced its worst evils.

Thirdly, this helps to demonstrate that, in the Christian view, the greatest evils are not physical, nor even psychological, but spiritual. That is not to try to shrug off physical and psychological suffering (Christ shared those too). But it is to say that, if we can't see any further than these, we miss one of the keys to understanding them. The basic trouble is spiritual evil and that is well epitomized in the apparently harmless, and even seductively attractive, rebellion of man against God. Physical and moral and all other kinds of evil follow from spiritual evil and will not be abolished until spiritual rebellion is at an end. The evil in the world is, in the Christian's view, all related to spiritual evil. The imperfections of nature arise out of the fact that the universe is no longer a harmony. Spiritual beings – notably man – exist in the universe at loggerheads with God and, as long as that is true, nature itself is disordered. In the Garden of Eden man's fall affected the natural world also. But the Bible presents us also with a picture of the devil active long before the creation of man. As the first book of the Bible introduces evil in this way, so the last book describes its exit as following only when all *spiritual* rebellion against God is eliminated.

The frightful evils that we see in the world are therefore seen by the Christian as either the result of man's disharmony with God, or as the indirect symptoms of some other kind of *spiritual* disorder. In disease, which is a small-scale but typical example of the whole problem, the symptoms are sometimes terrible but the disease itself is the real enemy. The symptoms (at least some of them) may be necessary in order to make us aware of far greater evils in the background. If there were no symptoms for a disease, but only a secret growth of bacteria in the blood until we lapsed into unconsciousness, the illness would be extremely difficult to diagnose and to treat. In fact the trouble with cancer is that it frequently has too few painful symptoms early on. That is why it kills. Pain in moderation is something for which we should be most grateful. It is a marvellous and sensitive early warning system, though we do not deny that pain can reach a level where it is a vile evil, destructive of all that is human, and clearly every effort must be made to alleviate it long before that point is reached.

Now if it is true that all human physical and mental suffering are only a little thing in comparison with spiritual evil, then we can press the analogy with disease and talk of such suffering as a mere symptom of evil and so as a warning system – a constant reminder that this life is fallen and in need of desperate remedies to put it right. Spiritual evil is not entirely hidden, nor entirely spiritual in its results, and for that we should be *thankful*. Its symptoms constantly stir us to action against the real enemy. Typical of all real evil is the fact that its side effects in physical evil fall so unevenly and hit hardest at some of those who least deserve it. We do right, therefore, to see in it the activity of a vicious and malevolently evil being. If we have seen such evil do its worst we cannot laugh about it – or him. But at the same time we must be thankful that the world is so ordered that we can identify and attack the real enemy (*spiritual* evil in man and in the devil) even while we also give our energies to healing the wounds and limiting the symptoms.

This position is of course unacceptable to those for whom the greatest good is to be found in present pleasure. But the Christian sees that position as tragically superficial and blind both to the greatest good and to the greatest evil. Because such people can attack only the symptoms their efforts are always extremely short term even from the point of view of this life.

Finally, then, this pushes us back to the ultimate question. Why does God allow the world to be like this? Why, for the purpose of eternal good, does he allow temporary but violent and vicious evil to mess up the whole creation? The Christian knows that all evil will in the end be overcome and destroyed. He knows that there is to be a new heaven and a new earth which are ruled by right and in which there will be no pain or suffering or evil of any kind. But why does God allow it, and suffer it himself, for the present? We keep on asking whether he could not have done it another way.

Now it does not seem to me that we have any complete answer to that question. We can philosophize about it to some extent. We can show that if God has made beings with such a colossal capacity for harmony, that in itself implies the capacity for discord. An old piano is no substitute for an orchestra in which skilled players can get far, far more out of their instruments. But the orchestra is capable of far worse noises than a piano. It does seem that the possibility, but not the fact, of evil is probably inherent in the possibility of good.

God created such a situation that real harmony and beauty are possible. The lower organisms have some capacity for sensitivity and a correspondingly limited capacity for suffering, for instance. The higher animals have great capacities for both. However we justify it, it does seem that, in the world as we know it, the greatest and best things imply the possibility of their opposites. In particular we can see that love ceases to be love if it is merely a forced response. The whole point of true love is that it is spontaneous, a genuine appreciation of the other, and something that we *need* not have given. God made man vastly higher than other terrestrial creatures in that he can love God. That involves quite obviously the possibility (not the fact) that men might fail to love God and rebel. A being who could not do otherwise would be a machine and would not be showing real love.

At this point some writers attack the Christian position by saying that in that case God is not omnipotent. If he really were omnipotent he could do anything. He could have created beings capable of real love and also incapable of evil, or who did not in fact ever choose evil. But if that is true, then God preferred to do it another way because in the long run it is far, far better, even if, in the short run, it seems worse. The Christian may simply have to trust that God knows best. In practice, however, the more people value spiritual and eternal things the less the problem becomes, even when they personally or their loved ones suffer. It is those who deny that there could be anything worse than physical and mental suffering who find the problem most difficult because they have no perspective by which to judge it. Yet the people who shout loudest here are often extremely inconsistent. Often they justify creating suffering deliberately by means of violence for the sake of some this-worldly ideal. If they allow that that is good they cannot complain if God allows some evil for a while for the sake of a far higher and *eternal* good.

But to say that God can do anything does not mean that he can deny himself and his own moral nature. Christians in fact hold that God 'cannot' – or perhaps we could say equally well 'will not' – do that. He is consistent. At least as we look at it from a human point of view he does not make black and white, good and evil into the same thing. We should not try to make God's activity into self-contradictory nonsense. God is able to do all that is in accordance with his perfect nature and, baffling as it is, that apparently does include allowing evil some scope for a short time and turning it to ultimate good before it is eliminated. It is not self-evident that there could be another way of doing it. Most alternatives involve sheer self-contradiction and nonsense. The problem is tied up with the question of what it means to be a man 'in the image of God'. Apparently that includes the possibility of being in rebellion against God. Its object is that we might love, and enjoy, and serve God, but it casts the sinister shadow of its opposite as a possibility. God is not to be blamed if we turn it into an all too present reality. He foresaw it, of course, and judged that it was worth it; but he is not responsible for evil.

We must leave the subject here. I hope that enough has been said, however, for the purposes of this book. I have tried to show the falsity of the charge that from nature we must infer an imperfect or impotent God if we infer God at all. We said that the problem appears to the non-Christian to be acute only for the Christian. But we have shown that from inside the circle of a Christian world-view the problem is not in fact so acute. From the inside spiritual evil is the great evil and all other kinds are only a symptom of the disease. The evil in nature is not an embarrassment to the Christian if he has come to terms with the fact of spiritual evil and the possibility that this is inherent in the possibility of spiritual good.

To many non-Christians this is entirely unsatisfactory. Some of them are really deeply exercised about the enormity of evil. They want to scream against a God that allows it. At the same time they usually deny that there is spiritual evil and that it could matter more than anything else that men are rightly related to God. The non-Christian who feels moral indignation over the question has, however, another problem raised by the whole discussion. Why does he hate evil and pain and suffering so much? Can he really justify that hatred? Is he not here giving way to an almost instinctive sense of ultimate right and wrong for which there is no room in his philosophy?

Often this seems to be so. The very fact that men have a sense of good and evil is a witness to some standards outside themselves. The fact that their standards here agree with the revealed character of God is significant too. They are right to appeal against God on the basis of what little they know of God. But there is an answer when we accept God's revelation of himself. This hatred of pain and suffering and other forms of evil bears witness to the fact that man is a creature of God made in the image of God and unable, however hard he tries, to eliminate this trace of the damaged and distorted image. This in itself points beyond mere matter in motion to a meaning for life which cannot be thought of in terms of less than a personal God. The fact that man has a problem of evil shows that there are ultimate *moral* issues in the world as well as intellectual issues. In this sense it hints that the solution of the problem may be discovered in terms of relationship with God as the ultimate issue of life.

People cannot have it both ways. If there are no ultimate morals, then evil is not ultimately morally evil. It is unpleasant (or something similar) and that is about all. If, on the other hand, it is said that on the Christian view of God there is a terrible problem, then it must be open to the Christian to show that, on the Christian view of God and his world, the problem is not so acute after all because suffering is not so ultimate as the non-Christian might think. It is not possible logically to say that on the Christian view there is a problem which must be answered in terms of a sub-Christian estimate of God, of priorities, and of God's relationship to man. That however is the demand that most critics of Christianity are making at this point. From inside the Christian outlook suffering does make sense and evil is intelligible, even though we don't know all the answers. We must still be hushed with horror at many things in the world and respond by making a major effort to overthrow them; but evil is not an obstacle to belief in the Christian God, or to the belief that God's creation shows us something of his reality, power and character.

5. The meaning of human life

We have discussed two reasons for believing in the Creator and two chief objections to it. The fact of existence and the nature and harmony of the universe have been looked at briefly as reasons for faith; and the possibility that science explains it all away and the problem of evil have also been given some sort of an answer.

We come now to two further positive reasons which revolve round man himself. They can be called the wonder of man and the fact of morality. Professor Bronowski, in his elaborately documented TV series which is published under the title *The Ascent of Man*,[1] sees the chief differences between man and animals in terms of man's gift of foresight, his ability to postpone satisfaction of desires, his development of language, his long childhood, his being a 'solitary-social' animal, *etc.* All this can be accepted as valid and important biologically and sociologically. But the Christian is bound to say that it seems very superficial stuff compared with the differences that he is aware of. To the Christian man is primarily a being facing God. If he did not have these extraordinary biological and psychological capacities it would not be possible to think of a meaningful relationship to the Creator, but the point of these capacities is that they make him a being capable of a level of experience and existence which is different from that of other animals. The biologist all too easily loses the wood for the trees, even while he is full of wonder as he discovers the details. The Christian has to ask whether we can really think that man,

[1] B.B.C. Publications, 1973.

with his astonishing capacities, is just the product of lower order physio-chemical processes. Does he not imply a personal Creator greater than himself?

What a work of art is man!

Even if we think that the vast spaces of the universe and the whole range of living things may well be nothing more than a complex of purely impersonal forces in a universe that just happened, can we say the same about man and in particular about ourselves? Scientifically speaking, life may be just 'poor, nasty, brutish and short' but there is so much more to it than that. It has qualities that really do not seem to be satisfactorily thought about in terms of a mere concourse of atoms. The things we value most in human society and human relationships are just not the same kind of thing as a scientific equation although such equations are no doubt involved.

The problem is rather like that of a team of chimpanzees who had been taught to use typewriters. It has often been pointed out that if they worked long enough in a purely random fashion one of them would produce a Shakespeare Sonnet. That is presumably true, if they were given enough time, but of course the chimpanzee would not have 'written a sonnet'. He would have strung together some ink marks of no meaning to him. As far as he is concerned it would have no greater significance that a page of nonsense. If we came along and read it as a poem that would be because the programme was set up by some human being with this possibility inherent in it (a machine that can write words) and because men can see the sort of significance that arises from *words* on paper, not just ink marks on paper. Looking at man we have to say that the possibility of such a phenomenon as he is is most remarkable and that this tells us something about the nature of reality. There are levels of existence far above the mechanical, and these need to be explained not in machine talk (typewriters) but in terms of non-material realities (personal ideas).

How is it that material elements combined in certain ways convey such great potential of a personal kind? How is it that my neighbour is a person, able to respond to me? The fact that 'I am fearfully and wonderfully made' has prompted innumerable thinkers to believe that man has been made by a God who takes some special delight in the level of existence that man represents. Man is so wonderful that it is very hard not to believe that he has a meaning beyond mere physical existence. If it is hard not to see some pointers to God in the material universe it is far harder to avoid the idea that man points to a reality greater than himself and his world. 'What a work of art is man!' What levels of reality he contains! Can we be satisfied with views of his meaning which speak exclusively in terms of realities of a lower order than himself? However he arose (and that does not matter for the moment), man seems to ask for an explanation in terms of something greater than himself, in fact in terms of a personal Creator.[2] Alternative views of man are of course enormously varied. The modern Humanists, for instance, while they constantly assert that there is no God, are foremost in claiming that life has a meaning in terms of ideals. It is, they say, enormously worth while to try to improve the lot of man and to enrich life in every way we can.[3] This kind of outlook is far more common than the title 'Humanist', and it is worth discussing as one of the major alternatives to Christianity quite apart from the Humanist label.

[2] The apostle Paul at Athens reasoned with the philosophers that, as they really knew it was inadequate to think that ('We ought not to think that') man was created by idols (less than man), they ought to have gone beyond their religion to follow their awareness of a supreme Creator who is far greater than man. He went on to tell them that the Creator has come in the man Christ Jesus. But at this stage in our discussion the point is that it is unconvincing to explain man in terms of 'science' or idols or anything else less than man. Man calls out to be explained in terms of the Creator God.

[3] H. J. Blackham, for instance, in his book *Humanism*, starts with the sentence: 'Humanism proceeds from an assumption *that* man is on his own and this life is all, and an assumption *of* responsibility for one's own life and for the life of mankind – an appraisal and an undertaking, two personal decisions' (Penguin Books, 1968). The problem is how to hold both these assumptions at once.

Basically, however, this outlook is trying to have the cake and eat it. If there is no reality greater than man, if this life is all there is and man is merely a complex animal who both individually and collectively is bound for extinction, then how do we maintain these ideals? Why should we care for the next generation, for the environment, for culture? Why should I care for anything except that degree and kind of society that will make life pleasant for me? In an age when many are primarily and openly self-seeking it is a tremendous gain to society that there are those, both Christian and non-Christian, who care intensely for the good of mankind and of future generations. But these positive aims for which the Christian is bound to be most thankful can be satisfactorily justified only in terms of a meaning of human life that implies at least abstract ideals greater than man. When men stop to think about life they are constantly pushed towards some sort of transcendent ideals and transcendent meaning for life. This is not the place to argue it out in detail,[4] but the Christian would say that in this Humanists bear witness, without realizing it, to a personal Creator. What they describe in abstract terms the Christian affirms is one small and somewhat distorted aspect of the reality of God. When these ideals are examined in isolation they cannot stand on their own. They must either be regarded as intuitive, or self-evident, or in some other way valid without rational justification, or they must be regarded as deriving their validity from some transcendent reality such as God. Magnificent as it is (like the charge of the Light Brigade[5]) this kind of attempt to put meaning into life does not have the rational basis that it needs. As a Humanist spokesman once put it in a university debate: 'While granting that, on a Humanist view, life has no ultimate meaning, we must work hard to put meaning into life.'

[4] For a fuller discussion see C. G. Martin, *How Human can you get?* (IVP, 1973).

[5] This entirely futile and almost suicidal obedience to a mistaken command was described by a French General in the phrase 'It is magnificent. But it is not war.' To hold tenaciously to these ideals without adequate reason is magnificent but it is not convincing – especially to those who, like the Humanists, profess to be dependent on 'reason' alone.

But meaning cannot be conjured up out of nothing. There is intellectual 'smuggling' involved in holding transcendental ideals while denying the existence of any transcendental world.

The wide spectrum of 'Humanist' views may be called a 'weak' alternative to Christianity, because it is weak in intellectual justification and appears to many people to be an impossible compromise. It is today being increasingly replaced by a 'tougher' alternative – the 'Man is a Naked Ape' outlook. This is tough-minded in the sense that it is more mercilessly consistent. In its logically consistent form it amounts to this: If there is no God, then the universe has no purpose or meaning outside itself. All we can talk about are trends which have taken place through a combination of causes and effect (including, perhaps, ultimately random events). The universe therefore is meaningless and human life is meaningless. Events just happen and have no more significance than that.

This kind of view is becoming more popular; but it is extremely hard to maintain and that for two chief reasons. First, if it is to be held consistently it seems to deny the validity of all thought and argument as we have discussed on pp. 36f. If so, it is self-destructive. In practice also we find it impossible to maintain consistently. If we try to adopt a philosophy of meaninglessness as an outlook we find that we are still, all the time and for good reasons, lapsing into thinking as if life really had some ultimate value outside itself. For instance, it is not just traditional attitudes that make it hard to believe that death is totally the end. It is easier to maintain this in theory than at the actual graveside or standing beside the dead body. There are things about people – qualities which they possess – which at times provide strong hints of life having significance beyond biological life. Men and their influence are soon forgotten, but is death really the end? It is hard to believe that so magnificent a creature as a human being just snuffs out. This is not because of his physical capacities but because he is so evidently more than a mere body.

It is, however, life, rather than death, that is the strongest

59

ground for believing that man has a significance other than in terms of his own personal and social life. However jaundiced our view of human nature, and even if man is only a rotten tomato sailing for a short time through space, he does seem to be on a purposeful errand. We cannot fail altogether to think in terms of ultimate good and bad and ultimate meaning of some sort for our lives and the lives of others. Again and again we find our thinking slipping back into terms that require such a background even when we theoretically deny it and this is not because it is a lazy alternative or mere tradition; it is the pressure of experience that pushes us this way. The hardest-headed materialist still blames or praises himself and others for their action and attitudes. He still wants to be involved in altering the course of events. Sartre, the philosopher of nihilism, still could not avoid being personally enthusiastic for a political cause – to the horror of his more logically consistent supporters. His position was just too self-destructive to be true for real life. A logically consistent denial of all meaning to life (except in terms of itself) is too bad to be true in the sense that we cannot honestly live by it. It is too inadequate to be true, like calling a picture mere lead on canvas, but it also denies some of the very things that are part of what we know we are – what it means to be human and to be able to believe, even if it is only belief in materialism. It is not just that believing in God is comforting or makes life easier to live. If the alternative is a consistent denying of all meaning in life then we cannot rightly believe or know anything. Yet we do believe, even if we only believe that life is meaningless. We find it impossible to accept that even that belief is an illusion. I say 'impossible'. Historically of course people have argued for such a position, but the realities of life have forced them to live and think most of the time in quite another way. They have to be inconsistent with their philosophy in order to live.

To return to Humanism; that, by contrast, can be lived out. It has ideals and a scale of values, even though it cannot really justify itself intellectually. But a consistent denial of all meaning to life, though it may be logically consistent if there is no God, leaves us unable to live. We cannot construct an alternative society in which absolutely nothing matters in any ultimate sense. So much in life is determined by a scale of values and a sense that certain things are worth while. Even human happiness or pleasure are not adequate goals if life is only a meaningless concourse of atoms. When we stop and think about our lives we are pushed towards thinking that they mean something. And if they mean something then we have to say how that can be if there is no God who knows and cares what we are and how we live.

A moral universe

There is a further range of evidences which have been collected under the general title of moral arguments, but in my view most of them are not worth pursuing. There is one, however, that seems to be making an important and cogent point. This may be set out briefly as follows:

1. Man is a moral being and has a strong sense that some actions 'ought' to be done and others 'ought not' to be done.

2. This sense of oughtness cannot satisfactorily be reduced to a mere by-product of evolution or to any other impersonal basic concept. It seems to stand in its own right as a distinct aspect of reality.

3. It suggests strongly that man cannot help seeing himself as over against a God, or at least a super-human ideal, to whom or to which we have obligations. The fact that we have a moral sense is therefore a pointer to someone or something above and beyond man – some sort of transcendental moral reality.

It is probably not necessary to argue the point (1). The crux of the argument is in (2). One alternative solution that is popular today argues that morals are purely the result of society trying to reinforce the otherwise inadequate social cohesion in man. Ants obey the community without the need for any moral sense, as far as we know. Man does not do so unless his social behaviour is reinforced by conscience. We are told that what exactly is regarded as right and wrong

61

doesn't matter greatly. Society, however, has to have some rules and has to give them authority. By education and by some kind of subconscious, and possibly even inherited, conditioning man has developed a conscience and therefore behaves far more socially than he otherwise would. He is able to forgo personal gain for the good of the herd.

The trouble with this kind of alternative is that it proves too much. If it is right, then morality has no ultimate justification. It is merely a psychological trick played on us by an oppressive society. It is an opiate of the people. We have no need, for instance, to put the well-being of future generations above our own pleasure. After all, man may have destroyed himself before those generations are born and, in any case, by what standards can we say that anything 'ought' to matter *to me* more than my own pleasure? On this view my conscience is no more than a sort of psychological itch and if I can pacify it with drugs or psychotherapy I have no reason to allow it to spoil my pleasure. Yet most of those who argue like this want to maintain that we 'ought' still to serve mankind. It is the same sort of dilemma as that of the Humanist discussed on pp. 57ff. Either such a person has proved that ethics are a psychological cheat or, if he wants to maintain them, he has to bring in someone or something outside of man to do so.

This position is not altered for those who find a purely rational basis for morals. It is, in fact, similar to the case of our scientific understanding of the world. I am not saying that science, or ideals, or ethics are impossible without believing in God. Obviously they are possible. But, as in science so here, if we do not believe in God we are forced to provide an alternative explanation of the values and of the basis of the sense of ultimate right and wrong. If we deny God this seems to lead us in both fields into positions where we have cut off the branch we are sitting on. *Practical* ethical discourse can go on without agreeing about God or ultimate morality. The question I am raising however is: what kind of a universe is it that has as one of its ultimate aspects this moral sense?

There is here no proof, any more than in the other positive points we have mentioned. The fact is, however, that people do have moral experiences, and that, as a rule, they cannot honestly dismiss these as less than experiences of having obeyed or disobeyed a moral ultimate greater than themselves. When the Christian proposes as the explanation of these experiences the existence of a morally perfect God it makes extremely good sense. The awareness of having done right or wrong may (and should) be strongest when we can trace out the reasons for its being so in terms of its effects. But that does not mean that morals are 'nothing but' socially cohesive traditions. I am claiming that the experience of moral obligation points beyond itself to realities of another kind and that this is true whether our sense of obligation can be justified socially or not.

6. Awareness of God

In addition to these more or less objective arguments it has often been pointed out that a high proportion of men and women of all ages have had some sense of being confronted by God. It is not only that they believe intellectually that there is a God; they have at times some immediate, perhaps innate, awareness of a God who inspires awe, wonder, thankfulness and a realization of our moral inadequacy. Pascal expressed it as, 'The heart has its reasons that the reason never knows.'[1] It has both a positive and a negative aspect: an awareness of God which may make me want to run away and an awareness of my need for God. What does this represent? Is it merely a psychological hangover from our childhood with God as a substitute for a father-figure carried over into adult life? Is it merely a sign of inadequacy or does it correspond to some reality? If it is an irrational phenomenon, like fear of the dark, we ought to grow out of it. In that case it may belong to our infancy but it ought not to belong to adulthood.

I do not believe it is possible to show beyond doubt what this experience represents. The Christian explains it one way. It is open to the non-Christian to adopt any one of a number of alternative explanations so long as he finds them honestly convincing. They may of course be true as far as they go; but they must explain it all without residue if they are to exclude the Christian view. The father-figure substitute idea is weak because this religious sense is often strongest in childhood when no substitute is needed. But other explanations could be suggested.

[1] *Pensées*, 227: 'Le coeur a ses raisons que le raison ne connaît point.'

An innate sense of God?

Two comments are worth making, however. The four reasons for faith mentioned on page 24 give it a rational basis. You don't have to be a philosopher to look at the world and think that it points naturally to God. But you do have to be something of a philosopher to escape that perception, by showing that it is not proved by mathematical logic. The wonder and complexity of the creation does, therefore, make us aware of God quite reasonably. It is not something altogether irrational. It is a response on a broad level to the facts of innate experience. Since these facts are with us all the time this sense of being confronted by God is not easily dismissed as an illusion. Our fear of the dark has no rational basis. But our innate sense of God has, as we have tried to show, a very considerable rational basis.

Secondly, the Christian explains it in a way that is at least plausible. According to the Christian view man was made for fellowship with God. If he is not rightly related to God then there is something basically missing. He is aware of a sort of vacuum. His life is ex-centric and we would expect all sorts of frictions and problems to arise. Amongst these it is not unreasonable to expect an awareness of the fact that the solution for many of these problems might be a right relationship to God. Jesus Christ and his disciples spoke of a hunger and thirst which he said that he alone could satisfy. Augustine put it in the phrase:

'Thou Lord hast made us for Thyself and our hearts are restless until they find their rest in Thee.'

There is a danger here. Christians have sometimes spoken as if those who are aware of any kind of vague, personal deficiencies should rush into Christianity in the confidence that all problems will be solved. That is not true. To speak in this way is to raise false hopes. We have to be sure first what the trouble is. To run to Christianity in the search of psychological peace is dangerous and can be very disappointing. We must carry out a proper diagnosis before we try out cures. 'Religion' could even make things worse if the symptoms from which we want release are really symptoms

5

of something quite different. For example, a depression due to vitamin deficiency or physical disease could be aggravated by religious introspection of the wrong kind. On the other hand, if we discover that a part (and if so it is the fundamental part) of our trouble is that we are estranged from God, then it is only sensible to seek to have that put right. It may not solve our psychological problems; but in exploring a small disorder (or a new joy) people do sometimes discover this innate awareness of a God whom they do not yet know personally. Indeed, such awareness may arise in any way and at any time.

The Christian believes that there is a reality in this awareness of God which, although its diagnosis is not inescapable, is in fact an effective stimulus to many to seek God further, so as to try to discover if he is there and if he cares for men. It rests on the evidences which are around us but it comes into consciousness often at a more emotional level; an awareness of a great and awe-inspiring reality, an awareness of a God making demands upon us which we want to resist, together with a hunger and a thirst which can be satisfied only by a right relationship to God.

Why are some people unconvinced?

I have tried to set out certain grounds for believing what the Christian maintains is a fact: that there is a Creator God who confronts us in our experience of his creation. I do not believe that these amount to a proof. It is clearly possible for people of integrity to deny it. If the Christian is right, how can that be so? In particular how is it that philosophers, who have discussed these problems in the greatest detail, still often remain unconvinced?

Earlier we compared the situation to a picture-puzzle in which a face is hidden in the trees. All that we can do with the child who refuses to believe that there is a face there is to try to sketch it out once more and help him to 'see' it. Once he has seen it he is likely to lose it only momentarily. The philosopher's difficulty is often that he is looking for the wrong thing. This is accentuated in modern philosophy. He tends to break the problem down too small and to lose the whole in studying the parts. A face has to be studied as a whole. Each part could, in isolation, be something else. The eye could be a hole in the tree and the mouth a twig. The philosopher is also often asking for proofs of the wrong kind. He often wants strict, mathematical-style demonstrations and these are not available. The philosopher has got to be willing to look at it in more normal human ways.

When we do that we are confronted with a far from irrational awareness of God. Man and women are not in the position of having a blank mind on which evidence for God has to be written. They do have an experience which I have argued should be described as *awareness* of God. This arises both from their own inner experience and from the world around them. Men have responded to this in one of two ways. Some have taken vigorous avoiding action and have suppressed the knowledge they have. In some cases it amounts to repression, so that the awareness of God is pushed into the sub-conscious. This is not to say that those who do this are consciously dishonest. All repression and much suppression take place without continuous, conscious choice. When truths come up at us which for some reason we do not like, this is one possible response. Our psychological machinery pushes them into a position where we are either totally unaware of them or largely so. The classical case in the psychology books is sex. In a previous age that treated sex very negatively some people so suppressed it (or even repressed it) that they ended up almost sex-less. And yet, of course, it continued to work in their sub-conscious and came out in dreams and distorted symbols, *etc.*

Almost exactly the same can happen with our awareness of God. It should not be surprising, therefore, if it reappears in distorted forms, even in our much vaunted scientific age. We have, for instance, the increasing cultivation of spiritism, the extraordinarily wide-spread interest in astrology, an almost equally common faith in mascots, and the obviously 'religious' aspects of some anti-religious or political enthusiasms. This process can be described in less psychological

67

terms. Many people suppress the truth that they know inwardly, but this fails to eliminate religion. The religion they have is then often irrational because they have refused the only rational bases for belief in God. They escape the Creator and end up with an 'idol' – some distorted and fairly obviously inadequate God-substitute. Very few people end up totally 'irreligious' in the sense of having no transcendental or supernatural faith.[2]

The other main response is to admit that it *is* the Creator God of whom we have become aware. After accepting this conclusion, however, there is the greatest variety of decision as to what should be done about it. To many people it remains just one of those factors of life which we take for granted and allow to be little more than a part of our intellectual furniture. In all ages there have been people who have accepted the fact and reality of a Creator yet have lived intensely irreligious and anti-social lives. What they believe seems to affect them not at all. They are like the devils who also believe there is a God, except that, unlike the devils, they rarely even tremble. Of course it should not stop there; and to many a realization of God as Creator is the starting point of a path to personal faith and a complete re-orientation of life. If there is a Creator we want to know him – if he can be known.

Several of the points we have mentioned are commonly answered in terms of there being some abstract ideals or ideas which could make sense of our intellectual and moral search for meaning. People protest that, in introducing the idea of a personal God, we go too far. There may be some

[2] A large part of the argument of this section is based on the pithy sentences of Paul's letter to the Romans (chapter 1): 'Ever since the creation of the world his (*i.e.* God's) invisible nature, namely, his eternal power and deity, has been clearly perceived in the things that have been made.' 'What can be known about God is plain to them, because God has shown it to them.' 'Men . . . suppress the truth.' 'They did not see fit to acknowledge God.' 'Claiming to be wise, they became fools.' 'They exchanged the truth about God for a lie and worshipped and served the creature rather than the Creator.' Then, speaking of morality, he says of pagans: 'Though they know God's decree that those who do such things deserve to die, they not only do them but approve those who practise them.'

ultimate meaning in life and in society; there may be some irreducible moral obligation; there may be some great mystical reality which is a part of the universe. People are willing to make a substitute for the traditional idea of God in terms of 'Nature', or 'Evolution', or 'Life', or a large number of other alternatives. Why, they ask, make it a personal Creator? The Christian has to reply to this that these partial glimpses of a metaphysical reality are admittedly unclear to our limited and unwilling minds. Left to ourselves we would not arrive at a clear idea of God, as the variety of religious and mystical philosophies bears witness.

We must admit, also, that most of us have not really tried very hard to go any further. Jesus promised that those who seek will find. Our chief trouble is that we do not honestly seek in anything like the way that the subject demands. We may be willing to discuss but we are not always willing to be faced by God. There are other troubles too. We search for God while wearing distorting spectacles and insist that God takes forms that appeal to us. It is not necessary to analyse here all the barriers that men put up and that we all to some extent experience. What we do know, however, if we are Christian, is that we were enabled to see and that we now cannot shake off the realization that God is behind the natural order. Most Christians did not see it for some time or, if they saw it, did not respond. Then the truth became too plain and powerful for them to resist. That provides no basis for any sense of either intellectual or moral pride, but it does force us to a confident faith. It means that while no-one can be merely reasoned into faith, all men should be asked to face the evidence as honestly as they can.

The Christian says, however, that God has astonishingly enough gone much further. He has spoken and he has come in Christ, and now it all fits together. The Christian sees that the whole picture is not just a pattern; it is a face. These things all make sense in terms of God in a way that they cannot in terms of any other concept. That is why we must go on to the next section. So far we are bound to find the story incomplete although, we maintain, it is perfectly clear if only people will see it.

Summary of Part One

The points we have raised in this first section can be brought together like this. The very existence of the universe, and its extraordinary harmony and unity, lead many people to believe that it has a personal God as its Creator. Man himself in his extraordinary 'higher capacities' persuades many that they cannot do justice to their experience unless they think in terms of such a God. The fact that man is a moral being with a sense of obligation to someone or something greater than himself is a special aspect of these 'higher capacities' which goes even further, suggesting relationship to God. These all converge and lead the majority of people to the concept of a personal Creator. They do not prove it, but looking at the picture as a whole most men and women do at times glimpse the picture of a personal presence in the complex web of their experience of the world. At times this comes into consciousness as a conviction that there is a personal God – a sense of awareness of God. At other times we forget it or ignore it.

We believe that the logic of the position is as follows. God is not proved, but we are, or have been, aware that he is there. When all the weakness of the detailed arguments have been agreed we still find that, taking the picture as a whole, we are confronted by him. We are faced by a reality that *could* prove to be the personal Creator. We have more than a suspicion that he is a personal and moral God. If that is so, we ought at least to try to discover more. It could be that that God cares for men and for men individually. It could be that my moral failures can be dealt with. If these indications of God are right perhaps he has revealed himself further in other ways.

At the same time such knowledge of a Creator as the natural world can supply leads many people simply to be frightened of God. We may want to run away rather than to seek further. Many 'nature religions' are religions of fear whose main concern is to appease an angry or temperamental God. Such glimpses as man gets of God's wisdom, beauty and love are often obscured by awe and a sense of moral inadequacy. The great non-Christian religions often forget almost everything else. As we have pointed out, the marvellous harmony of nature and the extraordinary qualities of man lead many to think of God as having a positive concern for us; but that is easily lost sight of. The problem of pain and other aspects of the world leave us baffled to know how we can go further and become more clear about God.

The Old Testament interprets to us the world of nature. It does much more than that, of course, but it is not until we come to consider Jesus Christ that the whole picture becomes clear. Jesus shows plainly, what nature may be felt only to hint at, that God loves men and has actually been willing to come among men to help them. This shows us not only what God is like, it shows us his attitude to us. Fear becomes tempered with gratitude and love. If we realize at all that God is our Creator and Sustainer, we must approach him with awe. But in Jesus Christ we see that he can be approached with humble confidence. A lifetime of study of the evidence for God in the creation will never bring us to the truth made plain and intelligible in Jesus Christ. Therefore we must go on to the next section before we try to form an integrated picture of what may be known about God. There is enough in what we have discussed so far to mean that we are under a serious obligation not to let the matter rest. We ought to seek further. If we do not we are to blame and are in danger of slipping back into a suppression of truth.

Part Two
The fact of Jesus Christ

7. What was Jesus like?

When all has been said about the evidence which we find in the natural order for the Creator it comes as something of a jolt to start talking about Jesus Christ. Yet that is exactly what we must do, and he confronts us in an almost abrupt way. He seems to rise out of the sea of history like a stark and jagged rock apparently having no connection with anything else. But when we examine the question further, we find that there are plenty of connections and that the fact of Christ is the key to understanding the rest. It is not essential, however, to trace all these connections now. We can just consider the person Jesus Christ. Whether we like it or not, we have in all honesty to give some sort of answer to the question of who Jesus is and what he signifies. The bare figure in history demands our attention. The connections begin to appear as we go along.

The New Testament preachers were not embarrassed to put side by side in the same address the fact of God seen in nature and the fact of God's complete revelation of himself to men in the apparently altogether different mode of the person of Christ. If the natural order points to the Creator, the person of Jesus Christ makes the revelation plain. Here God has done more than leave us to make inferences. God has, as it were, become an object in history for our examination, not only in general trends and overall impressions but in a particular person at a particular time and place. The claim is that here God has come himself because he loves us.

That the claims of Christianity should focus in Christ has seemed to many people improper. Some feel that the basis of faith should be general, philosophically convincing and couched in abstract terms. To them revelation in a particular person is a scandal. Others feel that, if there is to be personal revelation, then it ought to be in a chain of prophets each speaking into their own generation and culture. There are in fact innumerable ideas as to how God *ought* to have revealed himself. But such philosophizing is even less likely to be a sure guide than the philosophizing that led the professors of Padua to refuse to look through Galileo's telescope. We have first of all to allow God to speak as he sees fit. The Christian claim is that God was in Christ reconciling the world to himself and that, although there have been many prophets and many partial revelations, here, in Christ, God himself comes and speaks uniquely and completely in a way that cannot be repeated or imitated. That is the claim of Christ himself as we shall show, and it has to be faced and either accepted or rejected.

At this point some people object that we surely ought to be persuaded first that God exists and then we can discuss whether Jesus Christ is the revelation of God. But that is not at all necessary. In fact for many people it is only when they are confronted by Jesus that the idea of God takes reality. They begin to see what it means to talk about God when they see what kind of a person Jesus is. The idea of God may well be exceedingly vague until this happens to us. Both the idea of God and many of his characteristics are settled at once when we see who Jesus is. The whole truth of Christianity hinges on this. We ought now to start looking at the data. It is extremely easy to hold false ideas of what in fact Jesus was like and of what he said and did. The best remedy is to read a Gospel, either at one sitting or in large chunks. All of it, of course, is worthy of detailed study; but any reader of this book who has not done so fairly recently is urged to take the time for a quick reading through before going on. Here we can take only a few incidents from the Gospels.

His character

John, in the introduction to his Gospel, summarizes the character of Jesus as 'full of grace and truth'. This is how Jesus' closest disciple puts it. He goes on in the same sentence[1] to say, 'we have beheld his glory, glory as of the only Son from the Father.' The writers of the Gospels tell us that, when a man confronts the life of Jesus, he sees the glory of God's character as far as it can be expressed in a man. The picture of that glory starts with details of Jesus' relationship with people and conversations with individuals. As the story proceeds these details fit together into a most compelling unity in which grace and truth stand out. We are shown how, almost from the first, people were divided in their attitude to Jesus. As soon as they began to appreciate his claims and his power they began to be moved either to faith or to a growing opposition to him. His truth was too uncomfortable and demanding for many; his grace overcame the stiffest resistance in others. By 'grace' John means not only graciousness of character but the outgoing mercy of God to those who deserved the opposite. It starts with his care for the individual, his care for the nobodies of the day including women and children, his active help for the most vulgar sinners (such as business racketeers, who simply make us angry), his patience with those who were so slow to see the point or deserted him in the time of need. Above all there was his willingness to give himself to suffer and die for people who were still almost entirely unappreciative, rude, condescending or even fiercely hostile. For this he gave everything. Grace is personified in Jesus and came to its climax in his death for the undeserving.

At the same time Jesus was the personification of truth. He taught truth. But he also spoke out fearlessly no matter who was present; unless he could bring the truth home better by refusing to speak – as to the altogether venial ruler Pilate who was looking only for excuses. He was moved to indignation by the gross misrepresentations of God which were part of the current religious thinking so that he scath-

[1] John 1: 14–18.

ingly denounced the self-righteous and even drove the religious mercenaries out of the temple. He certainly taught truth and today the influence of that teaching is world-wide. But as we have said that was only a part of it. In himself he represented truth concerning God – who he is and what he is like – and concerning man – what he should be. He not only taught truth, he could say that he was the truth. He not only taught the way to God, he was the way to God. So he could say to his disciples, 'I am the way, and the truth, and the life.'[2] He makes it plain that truth is not just theoretical. In the end truth is personal. We have to think of the universe and its meaning in personal terms of which he is the apex and epitome. He came to turn grace and truth into personal relationship – a way to God and not merely a way of enlightenment.

These are two of the great descriptions of Jesus Christ. The disciples had no doubt that if we really understood who he was we too would realize these things and begin to see in them something of his unique glory. The character of Jesus Christ defies condensation into a few sentences, of course, but we have to start somewhere. Grace and truth are an admirable beginning. But now let us examine some of the incidents in Jesus' life to see what these meant in practice.

Who can forgive sins?

The Gospel writers obviously regarded as particularly important a happening early in Jesus' active public life when he returned to Capernaum from a preaching tour. The word got around that he was back at his base and a crowd gathered to see and hear him. The house became so packed that many could not get in and had to be content with listening round the door. At that juncture a paralysed man, carried by four friends, was brought to Jesus for healing. They could see that it was quite hopeless to try and push in through the door so they went up on to the roof, removed some of the

[2] John 14: 6.

roofing, and lowered the sick man down on his pallet in front of where Jesus stood.

No doubt there was annoyance at this distraction from the teaching that Jesus was giving, but Jesus, seeing their faith, turned to the paralysed man and said: 'My son, your sins are forgiven you.' No visible change took place. The man remained paralysed. If there was annoyance before there was consternation now. Some of the religious authorities were in the room and were immediately shocked at the implication of what Jesus said. 'Why', they said to themselves, 'does this man Jesus talk like that? It is blasphemy. He is claiming to be able to do what God alone can do – to forgive sins.' Jesus realized what was going on; probably he had said it deliberately so as to raise the issue. So he turned to them and asked, 'Why are you questioning what I have said? Which is easier to say to a paralysed man, "Your sins are forgiven you" or to say "Arise, take up your pallet and walk"?'

Now the answer to that question was fairly evident. Almost anyone could say the former and nothing visible would happen. No-one in fact would know if it was true. But very few people would dare to say to a paralysed man, 'Arise, take up your pallet and walk', because if nothing happened you would look a fool. So Jesus continued: 'But that you may know that I have power on earth to forgive sins I will say the harder thing also.' And turning to the paralysed man he said, 'Arise, take up your pallet and walk'; and the man got up immediately, took up his pallet and went out. It is recorded that they were all amazed and glorified God saying, 'We never saw anything like it.'

It seems clear that Jesus deliberately said these things in this order to show, though not to prove, that when he offered to forgive sins it was true. As his critics had said, that is something that God alone can do. Jesus in fact healed the man in such a way as to show that he had come for far more than ethical teaching or physical healing. The way he dealt with the man gave more than a hint of a claim to deity, and of a deity who was acting now to deal with sins.

Are the Gospel records reliable?

The story of course raises also the question whether the Gospel records are to be trusted. If one starts to work from incidents such as this people quite naturally retort that they cannot assume the reliability of the text. We must consider this briefly because it is basic to our further discussion.

We want to propose that the Gospels can and should be accepted by non-Christians not necessarily as reliable in detail, but as at least honest attempts to say what happened. There are four reasons for this. First, if we take the incident we have just related for instance, the subtle order of events is such that, if this is not a substantially correct account of what happened, it must be a very clever and deliberate fiction. This latter alternative is very hard to accept, for it involves the Gospel writers in wholesale fiction either because they were dishonest or because they were quite careless of truth. It is possible to suggest that the criteria of truth in those days were different and to point out that, in any case, the same sort of obsession with detail that has come in with a scientific age may well have been quite foreign to them. But we are not talking about detailed accuracy in the minutiae of the story. That is another discussion into which we need not go. What we are pointing out is that the story *as a whole* has a clear message. Either Jesus unmistakably laid claim to being able to forgive sins or he did not. The Gospel writers say that he did in this rather subtle way. Unless they were dishonest men something like it must have happened.

Secondly, Luke at least explicitly claims to have done some careful research and to be recording only what he was satisfied was true. Compared with the other Gospel writers he refers often to contemporary history. He was not indifferent to accuracy and, wherever we can cross-check, he turns out to have been an extraordinarily shrewd and reliable historian even in detail.

Thirdly, almost everyone agrees that the Gospels were written within about 30–40 years (or in the case of John at most 60 years) of the events. That is to say, they were recorded within the life-time of a very large number of living witnesses, both friendly and hostile. Even in our age of books and magazines many people have no difficulty in remembering pretty accurately events that happened 60–70 years ago. (If the reader doubts that, he had better go and talk to some old people, and check their reminiscences of striking events.)

The Gospel writers also seem to have had no qualms about the possibility of being contradicted. The only thing they mention that was disputed was the resurrection of Christ. Here they tell us that a story was circulated to the effect that the disciples stole the body while the soldiers slept. It seems likely that, for the rest, their account of things was not seriously questioned. And why should it be? There was no particular reason to question it if a great many people still living knew that it was substantially correct. The disputes, we gather, were not about the facts and teachings that they recorded but about whether the claims of Christ were true. Probably no-one doubted that he had made these claims and done these miracles and had taught the things that the Gospel writers say. It was only some time after, when all the eye-witnesses were out of the way, that people could attack the records. In all the violent disputes between the early Christians and the Jews, many of whom had been eye-witnesses, the disputes are not about the facts (not even as a rule about the resurrection) but about the meaning of the facts. Peter on the day of Pentecost, apparently without any fear of contradiction, said to the unbelieving crowd that they well knew the events of Jesus' life and death but had failed to see the point, partly because they didn't realize that Jesus was risen again. He didn't need to argue or even repeat more than an outline of the facts recorded in the Gospels. The emphasis in his sermon is on the meaning of these facts. We are several times told that Jesus' enemies could not deny his miracles and therefore resorted to saying that he did them by demonic power.

Fourthly, we would have to doubt the integrity of the whole early church. To an appreciable extent the four Gospels are independent. All agree in the substance of what Jesus did and taught. It is very hard to believe that they all lied deliberately, particularly when one of the great efforts of the early church was to teach people to tell the truth. Can they have lied in order to teach others to speak the truth? The time between the writing of the Gospels and the events which they narrate was too short for a Jesus 'myth' to have arisen. That requires generations. The whole witness of the early church was either culpable lies or honest reporting of events. It cannot be innocent myths.

It seems certain, then, that they *tried* honestly to say what happened and that we have adequate reason for reading their records as *honest* accounts. Many people feel unable to accept them as accurate in detail. But it should be possible to agree that they are honest and that they have succeeded in telling us substantially what happened. Even if we don't accept the detail, this gives us more than enough to go on with. The points we want to make do not depend upon being able to rely on every phrase and detail. It has often been pointed out, also, that, if we are unsure about the historicity of the apostles' description of Jesus, we have somehow to explain the fact that simple and uneducated men 'created' such a character and portrayed him with the most brilliant realism. Clearly these men had sat at the feet of one whom they recognized as quite unique; someone who, in ways that they explain to us, gradually showed himself to be the unique Son of God and not merely a great human teacher. It is hardly conceivable that they invented or imagined such an influential character.

There are, then, more than sufficient grounds for accepting the Gospel records as giving us a picture of Jesus Christ that is basically true to the facts.[3] That does not in itself, of course, drive us to faith. As we hope to show later, there can be no real doubt that Jesus claimed deity, but that still leaves open the question of whether that claim was true. Our discussion so far does not in itself settle this crucial question at all.

[3] For a much fuller and technically competent discussion see F. F Bruce, *The New Testament Documents* (IVP, 5th ed., 1960).

8. The methods Jesus used

The indirect approach

One of the really important things about any great leader is his method of communication. We want to know how he convinced people. Was it by the force of a hypnotic personality, by bullying, threatening, offering unrealistic rewards or what? Jesus' methods were consistent with his aim, which was to bring people to genuine personal conviction and faith of a kind that could stand the stresses of life. An incident which is recorded for us early on in John's Gospel provides a good example.

Jesus and his disciples were travelling back from Jerusalem to Galilee and passing through the somewhat hostile Samaritan area on the way. At noon they came to a well outside a Samaritan village and the disciples left Jesus alone and went to buy some food. While he waited one of the village women came out to fetch water and Jesus asked her to give him a drink. The woman was astonished, for the Jews were very scornful of the Samaritans and it was extraordinary for a Jewish man to ask a favour of a Samaritan – and a woman at that. 'How is it', she asked, 'that you, a Jew, ask a drink of me, a woman of Samaria?' Jesus replied that, if only she understood the gift of God and realized who he was, she would rather have asked him for 'living' water and he would have given it to her. 'Sir,' she replied, 'you have nothing to draw water with, and the well is deep; where do you get that living water?' Jesus answered, 'Every one who drinks of this water will thirst again, but whoever drinks of the water that I shall give him will never thirst; the water that I shall give him will become in him a spring of water welling up to eternal life.' Either because she was baffled, or just frivolous, she replied, 'Sir, give me this water, that I may not thirst, nor come here to draw.'

At that Jesus abruptly asked her to go and call her husband. When she protested that she hadn't got one he answered that he realized that she had had five husbands and was now living with someone else. She was astounded, but she also seems to have been annoyed. So she started a religious debate. Should the Samaritans worship in Samaria or Jerusalem? Jesus answered her conundrum but then added that the time had now come when men were to worship God, not in any particular place, but in spirit and in truth. God is interested in genuine worship and he seeks men and women who will approach him in that spirit. Probably this was a pointer to the need for seriousness in such a matter. But it was also a new description of the nature of true religion: genuineness matters more than outward form or place. 'Well,' said the woman, 'I know that the Messiah (or Christ) will come. When he does come it will all be made clear.' Jesus said to her, 'I who speak to you am he.' She must have been staggered by this claim, but just then the disciples returned and the conversation was interrupted.

This by any standard is a very convincing piece of writing and, if it bears any resemblance to the truth, then Jesus brought the conversation round to a statement that he could do what no-one else could do. He could give eternal life, for he was the promised Messiah, and was replacing the whole paraphernalia of the religious worship of the day. He could satisfy the thirst for God which no-one else could satisfy.

This conversation is of a piece with Jesus' whole method of teaching. There were his parables, for instance. They did not teach anything explicitly and directly, but when and if you were willing to stop and think about them, their main point at least was clear. So it was here. The woman could have tossed off all that Jesus had said as mystical twaddle. In fact we learn that she didn't; but that was because she did stop to think and also come back for more. In the end we are told she did in fact become a believer. Jesus never forced himself upon people. He helped them to see who he was if they were willing to follow it up. He promised that those who *seek* would find. Here he made it plain that he was the divine Messiah come to bring the fulfilment of all true religion and to bring eternal life as an undeserved gift.

The place of miracles

Both in this incident and in the story of the paralysed man which we looked at in our last chapter, there were miraculous elements (the healing and the knowledge of the woman's past). If we are to get a clear picture of Jesus' methods we must ask what place miracles had in his life. They seem always to have been used indirectly and never to prove a point by themselves. When Jesus was asked to do a miracle specially in order to prove his claims, he refused. Nearly all his miracles were for the purpose of helping people in need. They were never arbitrary demonstrations of power. Two of the personal temptations that Jesus refused at the start of his ministry had in fact been that he should do spectacular miracles in order to gain public support and that he should do miracles so as to avoid personally the limitations and hurts of human life. But when it came to the needs of others he frequently did help miraculously, though usually only when he already found faith towards himself and could therefore help without creating the wrong kind of belief. For instance, he rebuked those who followed him because he had fed the five thousand and they wanted more free bread. They had misconstrued the miracle. His miracles were not going to be a short cut to comfort for his followers nor a means of solving problems which ought to be solved by human effort. They seem to have been always a spontaneous stretching out in response to need, especially to specific and believing requests for help. Being who he was he could hardly refrain, except when miraculous action would mislead, or develop a wrong attitude, or in some other way do harm. Sometimes, therefore, he delayed until a right attitude had developed or until the situation and the observers had changed. He refused to parade the miracles he performed and he often told people who were healed to tell no-one about it – probably because he did not want to be thought of primarily as a miracle worker. The miracles he did were nearly always secondary to the truth he was teaching – as in the two examples we have discussed.

Nevertheless the miracles were a help to greater and more articulate faith. Some were known only to the disciples and seem to have played their part in helping them to see who he was. When he and a few others were in a boat on the lake and a great and really dangerous storm arose the disciples were afraid and woke him with a protest: 'Do you not care if we perish?' Jesus stilled the storm with a word of command. We read that 'they were filled with awe, and said to one another, "Who then is this, that even wind and sea obey him?"' [1] The miracles proved nothing, but they were a dramatic indication of the entirely unique kind of person he was.

Jesus never argued that the miracles proved that he must be divine because otherwise he could not have done them. He acknowledged that some kinds of miracles could have been done by evil powers. But he did say that they were *one* of the witnesses to whom and what he was and this was seen as much in their moral quality as in their strangeness.

Jesus often refers, therefore, simply to his 'works' which include all his actions and not only the miraculous ones. When asked who he was he pointed equally to the miracles and to the fact that the poor had the gospel preached to them. We must not read back into the Gospel a concept of miracles as events which are *scientifically* impossible. No such concept was then available. To the people of the time they were seen as 'signs'. We could call them signposts. They are also called 'wonders' and 'mighty works'. They were astonishing, of course, but they proved nothing in themselves and were all of a piece with his teaching and his claims. If Jesus was who he claimed to be then 'wonders' and 'mighty works' were to be expected as examples of his love and power

[1] See Mark 4: 35–41.

and they are particular indications as to who he was. Being divine, he helped people as he could, and because his miracles were of that kind they were seen not only as a witness to his deity but as a witness to the fact that he was the personal and unique representative of the loving and holy God. His miracles were signs of his grace and glory.

Miracles were an integral part of his whole life. His moral perfection, coupled with his miraculous power, coupled with the way in which he used that power, coupled with his teaching all make a harmonious picture. It is hard to find categories to explain such a person if we do not invoke the personal God he spoke about. As the disciples said in astonishment, 'What kind of a man is this?'

9. The teaching of Jesus

People may object that what has been said in the last two chapters has taken little account of Jesus as a teacher. That, after all, is a major, if not the major, aspect of his work and much of the New Testament is taken up with it. Now it is true that Jesus taught on a great many subjects – God, man, morality, heaven and hell, the world and eternal life, to name a few. It would be wrong to try to summarize it all in a few pages. For our purpose, however, it is important and necessary to outline some aspects and we can draw nearly all of them from what has come to be known as 'The Sermon on the Mount'.[1] That in any case is one of the most influential pieces of moral and religious teaching of all time. It is a co-ordinated whole, and though its themes often appear elsewhere in the teaching of Jesus, here they are brought together and related to one another. It was clearly given, partly to explain Jesus' attitude and relationship to the Old Testament and partly to interpret these Jewish scriptures for the new situation created by his coming. It was also to contrast his teaching with the then current religion of the Pharisees.

A description of the Christian man

The sermon starts, however, not with a direct contrast with the Old Testament or with the Pharisees but with the famous 'Beatitudes' in which Jesus describes the Christian

[1] See Matthew 5–7.

man. The result is as devastating now as no doubt it was then. The Christian man is presented not as a self-confident and self-righteous person who is sure that God is on his side and everyone else is inferior. Jesus' ideal is the one who is aware of his spiritual poverty, aware of his sins, meek, hungry for spiritual progress and true righteousness, merciful, pure in heart, a peacemaker and, far from being in a position to lord it over others, is persecuted and misrepresented. At the same time he is the salt of the earth and light of the world. His influence for good will be widely felt.

This, Jesus emphasized, is not because we turn our back on Old Testament morality but because we apply it correctly, not only to our outward acts but also to our thoughts and inner attitudes, not only to murder but to hate, not only to adultery but to lustful looks. Transparent straightforwardness and not merely avoidance of explicit lies, going the second mile and not merely seeking justice and, finally, love even of our enemy – these are the true outworking of the moral law. The genuinely Christian man possesses inner virtues and has thus built outward rules into humble and gracious aspects of character.

In these two themes – Christian character and a Christian spirit – Jesus sets before us a searching statement of what we ought to be. If we are honest it is extremely uncomfortable. No wonder we are aware of our sin and hunger for righteousness. We know we are not like that. We may have kept the ten commandments but Jesus was insisting on far more. In fact he laboured the point repeatedly. A whole train of passages in Matthew's Gospel comes to a climax in his words: 'Out of the heart come evil thoughts, murder, adultery, fornication, theft, false witness, slander. These are what defile a man.'[2] The fault with man is not basically in his environment but in his 'heart'. Whenever we contrast ourselves with Jesus himself and consider seriously his teaching we are left convinced of being inwardly impure. The disciples felt it too. 'Depart from me,' said Peter one day in despair, 'for I am a sinful man, O Lord.' That was the

[2] See Matthew 15: 18–20.

cumulative effect of Jesus and his teaching after only a short time. People were gradually pushed to this if they did not react into the proud hostility of their own self-righteousness. There were some then, as now, who felt that really they were not too bad and he had no right to imply that they were. But Jesus we are told 'knew what was in man'. He sees through us as he saw through the Samaritan woman at the well.

This standard of Christ has, down the ages, been the backbone of Christian living wherever it has been taken seriously. Christian Pharisaism has been as common perhaps as Jewish Pharisaism partly because we dislike facing the music. But whenever people have gone back to the actual words of Jesus they have been left without defence. When it comes to other people we can think of extenuating circumstances. But we cannot honestly do so for ourselves. We know that our excuses are very thin and that the facts are as Jesus said. Our motives are not pure. Our desires are very easily and frequently corrupted. Out of our hearts do proceed evil things.

God's judgment and forgiveness

Now all this might be bearable if in Jesus' teaching it had not been coupled with what he said about God's justice and his punishment of sin. It is easy to forget that in the New Testament the main references to hell are in the teaching of Jesus. He gives far more space to it than did his disciples in their writings. This is really shocking to many people. But Jesus was perfectly confident that sin has its ultimate consequences. The Sermon on the Mount has this embedded in it: 'If your right eye causes you to sin, pluck it out and throw it away; it is better that you lose one of your members than that your whole body be thrown into hell.' It is in the Sermon on the Mount that Jesus spoke of the danger of hypocrisy and being ultimately excluded from God's presence. It is here that he represents God as saying to certain very religious people 'depart from me, you evildoers'. We cannot possibly cut this aspect out of Jesus' teaching however hard we find it to accept.

Now one of the chief reasons why we find ourselves unable to accept unpleasant truths is because we have no remedy for the things that are exposed. We speak freely and openly about all kinds of illness and accidents but when we come to incurable cancer we suddenly start trying to find euphemisms or circumlocutions. The reason is simply that there is no remedy. Many people similarly will not face the truth of God's just punishment of sinners like ourselves because they really can think of no remedy. It is too unpleasant to face.

Jesus, at the same time that he spoke so devastatingly of sin and its consequences, spoke also of God as a loving Father waiting to receive those who would 'come unto' him. This, of course, had been taught by others. The Old Testament writers have many references to it. But only in Jesus' teaching is it so clear and so conspicuously set alongside the gravity of sin and God's judgment. He was, from the start, offering men forgiveness. He established the truth of God as 'Father'.

To many people the understanding of Jesus' teaching follows a zigzag pattern as they move from fresh awareness of sin, and almost despair about it, to fresh awareness of the wonder and greatness of God's forgiveness. There is a kind of backwards and forwards movement during which both truths are grasped more deeply. Jesus put these deliberately together as no-one else had done. First, this was because he knew as no-one else did how great God's forgiving love was. He could therefore enable us to face sin in all its foulness. But, secondly, Jesus not only revealed God as the One waiting to forgive. As his teaching progressed, as we shall show later, he moved on to explain that his death was necessary if men were to be forgiven; that the price of forgiveness was his suffering and that he had in fact come to establish the basis of forgiveness – to give his life a ransom for many – rather than merely to teach what men ought to be and are not. He therefore had a right and authority to forgive sins as no man ever had; and because he could forgive he could, and did, speak scorchingly of sin and its punishment if unforgiven.

While, therefore, he emphasized the awfulness of sin and its consequences, he also offered to men forgiveness and eternal life. He showed that reconciliation to God was possible in a way that left no room for pride and created a new faith which made it possible to be assured of his loving care, without the least trace of presumption or Pharisaism, because it is all totally undeserved mercy from God. Yet only a realization of the gravity of sin helped people to accept that humiliating position of dependence on God's 'charity'.

All this brought Jesus on to a collision course with the religious leaders of the day. It was they, not the vulgarly wicked, who had him killed. Evil men, who knew they were wrong, heard him gladly and some became his best disciples. By contrast, initially at least, hardly any of the very religious people would join him. His religion went so against the grain and was so different from all the religions that men have developed. It treated the best and most religious deeds and movements as totally inadequate because defiled by sin. Men had to start all over again, therefore, and give up their supposed religious superiority and accept his unearned mercy. No-one had an advantage in this faith except those who knew they were wrong.

The way to eternal life

Yet not all the religious leaders were opposed. We have the account of a secret visit paid to him at night by one of the Pharisees, a man named Nicodemus.[3] This man came, it seems, sincerely to probe further as to who Jesus was. He started with a little speech in which he acknowledged that Jesus was a 'teacher come from God' and that 'God was with him'. In reply Jesus did not build on this apparently promising start. He rather bluntly told Nicodemus that he needed to be 'born again' by the Holy Spirit before he could either see or enter the kingdom of God. The man was

[3] John 3: 1–16.

obviously baffled and asked if this meant some miraculous physical process. He really didn't see the point. So Jesus explained and gave one of the most concise gems of his teaching. Being born of the Spirit he said means an inward change. It has outward effects, but it means the start of a new spiritual life – eternal life. God has to do something inside us. Then, and then only, are we really part of his kingdom. All the admiration for Jesus as a 'teacher' he swept aside as not even having begun to see the point. He was of course a 'teacher came from God' but if that had been all then he would have had little more to offer than other religious leaders.

Jesus, however, here claims that he has much more. He states that he has come down from heaven and knows about the truth uniquely. He offers now, in this life, an entry into eternal life. He offers forgiveness and freedom from the punishment of sin. He assures the man that God is far greater and more loving than the Pharisees realized – intensely religious though they were. It is summed up in the phrase: 'God so loved the world that he gave his only Son, that whoever believes in him should not perish but have eternal life.' The context and the language make it plain that he is talking about a personal trust in himself as the divine Saviour, not just an intellectual acceptance of his claims.

To explain things to Nicodemus Jesus used an analogy from Jewish history. He compared himself to the brass serpent that Moses had lifted up in the wilderness. In a time when the people of Israel had been suffering a plague of venomous snakes as a direct punishment for sin, Moses was told by God to make a brass serpent and lift it up on a pole so that all could see it. Then God promised that anyone bitten by a serpent and looking, just looking, to the brass serpent would be healed. It was one of the most vivid object lessons of God's principle of forgiveness. Here the Israelites were taught to believe that sin deserved punishment and would get it unless people were willing to accept God's entirely free and unearned offer of forgiveness. Jesus said that 'as Moses lifted up the serpent in the wilderness, so must the Son of man be lifted up, that whoever believes in him may have eternal life'. It may all seem a bit childish, but then we all are a bit childish – even the most sophisticated. At least this figure is intelligible even to children and not only to the philosopher and theologian. So Jesus said he was to be lifted up – a repeated reference to his future death on the cross – so that those who believed in him should, as the following verses say, 'not perish but have eternal life'. Believing is compared to mere looking; it is never regarded as a meritorious act of which we can boast.

This chapter goes on to a consideration of why, in spite of all that God offers, men will not have it. He doesn't force it on them as if they were automata. Jesus came, we are told, not to bring judgment on men but to save them. And yet, if people refuse the entirely free and unearned forgiveness and new life that God puts before them in Christ, they are judged by that very refusal. 'This is the judgment, that the light has come into the world, and men loved darkness rather than light, because their deeds were evil. For every one who does evil hates the light, and does not come to the light.'[4]

Once more we see Jesus expressing, in himself and in his teaching, grace and truth. The effect on Nicodemus at the time we do not know. It seems that he did not immediately believe in Jesus or we should probably have been told. But he reappears twice later. In the face of unreasonable hostility to Jesus and the remark by an official in front of the chief priests and Pharisees, 'Have any of the authorities – or the Pharisees believed him?' Nicodemus (himself a Pharisee) was bold enough to stand up and say that Jesus should at least not be condemned without a fair hearing. Again, when Jesus was dead, and a wealthy secret disciple came and took down the body to bury it, Nicodemus risked his entire reputation by joining him. He also brought extremely expensive spices to embalm the body and this was at a time when even the twelve disciples had run away. It seems that Jesus was not in a hurry at their first meeting. He didn't make it easy for the man to become a disciple but he laid the foundation for a faith which was as tough as that of the

4 John 3: 19, 20.

twelve. But that was his way as a rule. He set before people the truth in its starkest and also its most wonderful aspects. He told them that faith in himself was the way into right relationship with God, which is eternal life. He challenged them, but he did not over-persuade, and from that came the faith and the new life that revolutionized the individuals and the world.

10. Jesus' claims to deity

Jesus clearly lived, taught and acted in a way that drove people to ask themselves repeatedly who he was, and this is the basic question we also have to ask. He was obviously a man in the fullest sense – absolutely human. No-one doubted that. His enemies said that it proved that he was not the Messiah, since to be that he would have to appear suddenly from nothing. He was surely human. But he was unique and more than human in so many ways.

Who do you say that I am?

His life and ministry follow a pattern. At first his claims were mostly indirect and he did not say what the future held. He allowed people to see him in action and to listen to his teaching without asking them to make up their minds immediately. Then comes an incident at Caesarea Philippi which is clearly a turning point. After this the Gospel writers show that he taught things he had not mentioned before and the whole sweep of his teaching opens up. The final stages of his ministry were the last supper and the following discourse which was addressed entirely to the eleven faithful disciples. Then it all culminated in his death and resurrection followed by a short period before he left the earth spent in teaching the disciples.

The crucial incident at Caesarea Philippi is worth special attention. The incident describes a sort of Part I in the examinations which had to be passed before the disciples could go on to grapple with Part II. We are told that there came a day when he turned to his disciples and asked, 'Who do men say that I am?' He had lived and taught long enough for it to be time for people to take sides. He was now deliberately pushing the disciples to declare themselves. They answered that there was a great variety of views of him – such as that he was John the Baptist or Elijah come alive again or a reappearance of Jeremiah or one of the other prophets. Then he put the question to them directly, 'But who do you say that I am?' Peter answered, 'You are the Christ, the Son of the living God.'

Almost certainly this was the first time that the disciples had put their thoughts into words so decisively. They had been astonished at him, sometimes mystified, occasionally even baffled and taken aback by his failure to be what they expected him to be. Up to that time Jesus had never given them a clear statement of what he claimed, but he had lived and healed and forgiven sins and worked miracles and denounced false religion and explained the truth. He had shown how the Old Testament was really to be understood and applied. They had seen his character and were irresistibly drawn to him in spite of his sometimes sharp reproofs and tremendous demands. Now he asks them who he is and for the first time they acknowledge with confidence that he is the divine Messiah. The Messiah had been promised in the Old Testament. Every devout Jew looked forward to his coming. Peter goes even further, however, because the concept of the Messiah could be pretty vague or largely military in popular thought. Peter declares that he is the Son of the living God – a *divine* Messiah. He has seen that Jesus is more than man and is prepared to say so with conviction.

Jesus' reply is very significant. Firstly he congratulates Peter. 'Blessed are you, Simon . . . Flesh and blood has not revealed this to you, but my Father who is in heaven.' Jesus had deliberately not given the sort of proofs for his deity that would have made the conclusion an inevitable formality. He had left it open, and not many did believe. But Peter had been given the understanding. He had 'seen' who Jesus was and it was far more than a statement of formal theology. It

7

was a personal confession of trust and confidence. Jesus, however, went on, and in his famous words declared, 'On this rock I will build my church, and the powers of death shall not prevail against it.' For our purpose it doesn't matter whether the rock was a reference to the truth that Peter declared or to Peter as the first instance of a full believer in Jesus as divine Saviour. This was a great turning point. Now some at least really did believe in the essential sense of that word. Here we have the beginning and foundation of Christ's living church. Here we have what is also the heart of present-day Christianity.

Among the things which Jesus now began to teach was the fact of his approaching death. This was something he had not spoken about before, perhaps because until this basic faith in his deity was clear, such teaching would have confused the issue. Only now that they knew he was divine could they begin to see what his death could mean – that it was not just the inevitable end but the real climax of his coming, and that it would be not a defeat but a victory.

This event at Caesarea Philippi explains much else in the Gospels. As a rule Jesus didn't allow explicit statements of his deity. He never gave a talk or lecture explaining fully who he was. What he wanted was not mere orthodoxy – correct ideas – but personal love and trust. It is significant that, when later Peter had denied him and wanted to be restored, Jesus asked him, not, 'Do you still believe that I am the Messiah?' but, 'Do you love me?' Jesus went to the heart of the personal relationship and helped Peter (and us in turn) to see that what matters is personal trust, which grows into love, as we discover more fully all he is and has done for us.

Some explicit claims

There were, later on, rare occasions when he was more explicit. At the last supper, for instance, he told the inner circle of disciples about his unique relationship to the Father. When the disciples answered, 'Lord, show us the Father, and we shall be satisfied', Jesus said, 'Have I been with you so long, and yet you do not know (recognize) me, Philip? He who has seen me has seen the Father . . . Do you not believe that I am in the Father and the Father in me?'[1] But perhaps one of the most striking occasions is his final trial. Here it was because of his clearly understood claim to be equal with God that he was condemned (a fact which could hardly have been wrongly remembered or misinterpreted). On a number of occasions they had tried to arrest or even to stone him because of this 'blasphemy'.[2] Now when the various witnesses who were brought against him could not agree, the chairman of the court solemnly charged him on oath, 'Are you the Christ, the Son of the Blessed?' Jesus answered, 'I am; and you will see the Son of man (*i.e.* Jesus) seated at the right hand of Power, and coming with the clouds of heaven.'[3] At this the whole company agreed that he was worthy of death. It was obvious to their small minds that this was a scandalous claim to deity which was an insult to the Creator.

There really is no doubt at all that Jesus claimed to be the divine Messiah, equal to God and one with the Father, and there is no doubt that his disciples and his enemies alike realized that he made this claim and that his whole position depended on whether it was true. To his enemies it was incredible. To his disciples it was the great discovery which led them to worship him, as well as to admire and love and follow him as leader and teacher and Lord.

Jesus' claims as a whole

We have said enough to make some sort of summary possible and this may help us to see how it all fits together.

First, *Jesus claimed to be the Messiah*, as he did to the woman at the well. But he claimed more than a vague, popular Messiahship. He claimed to be the *divine* Messiah

[1] John 14: 8, 9, 10.
[2] See, *e.g.*, John 5: 18; 10: 33.
[3] Mark 14: 61, 62.

who came to fulfil all the Old Testament hopes and to bring in a new order. His first preaching is summarized by Mark as 'The time is fulfilled, and the kingdom of God is at hand; repent, and believe in the gospel.'[4] When he called himself 'the Son of man', it is clear that the Pharisees realized that this referred to an Old Testament divine saviour.

His collision with the leaders of the day started with his *authority*. It is constantly recorded that he astonished people by this. He had no theological training but he spoke about God and man with a calm confidence that was at once authoritative and yet free from pride. He spoke as one who knew that he was right, not as one who was trying to persuade others that he was right. He knew that he was not just another man like other men. He knew that his relationship to the Father was unique. He told them that he spoke always the words it was given him to say. It was not only as a teacher that he was authoritative; he had authority over men's eternal destiny. 'I know (my sheep), and they follow me; and I give them eternal life, and they shall never perish, and no one shall snatch them out of my hand . . . I and the Father are one.'[5] He had authority over demons and disease and over the forces of nature. He reproved a group of theologians with 'You are wrong, because you know neither the scriptures nor the power of God.'[6] It was with the same authority that he raised the dead. When he met the widow of Nain following the dead body of her only son to its grave he stopped the procession and raised the dead to life again. It needed only his word of command: 'Young man, I say to you, arise.'[7]

Then, in spite of his devastating moral teaching, *he showed absolutely no trace of being aware of personal sin.* In one incident he even challenged them with 'Which of you accuses me of sin?' and no-one would rise and make an accusation. In everyone else he created an awareness of sin, and most other great moral teachers have confessed their

[4] Mark 1: 15.
[5] John 10: 27–30.
[6] Matthew 22: 29.
[7] Luke 7: 14.

own shortcomings. But Jesus never acknowledged sin in himself. At first this scandalizes us, as it did his contemporaries. But then there is absolutely no pride about it. It happened to be true and Jesus accepted it as he expects us to accept it. 'He committed no sin; no guile was found on his lips,' says Peter.[8] Indeed the matter seemed hardly worth disputing. It is only when we think of the nature of his teaching and the sad history of the imperfection of his disciples all down the ages that we realize a little of what an astonishing claim it was. To be without sin *by his standards* is almost incredible.

Then we have to accept the fact that *he offered to forgive sins* (which God alone can do); he offered to give to men eternal life for the asking and not as the result of a sevenfold way of spiritual battle to the end of life. He explicitly claimed a unique relationship to the Father, to time ('Before Abraham was, I am'), to moral truth, to the salvation of men and to victory over the devil. He claimed that his position would be unique – as God. He foresaw the future of his own death and resurrection and the path of suffering and final victory of his church. He accepted the worship of men.

But perhaps even more remarkable is *the apparent egocentricity of his teaching.* To those who talked about hunger he said, 'I am the bread of life; he who comes to me shall not hunger, and he who believes in me shall never thirst.'[9] To those who asked, 'What must we do, to be doing the works of God?' he replied, 'This is the work of God, that you believe in him whom he has sent.' Again in an appropriate context he answered, 'I am the light of the world; he who follows me will not walk in darkness, but will have the light of life.' There is much more of this, culminating in his great statement to the disciples, 'I am the way, and the truth, and the life; no one comes to the Father, but by me.'[10] His whole teaching centres in the fact that he was God the Saviour come to save men. He therefore led them to faith in *himself* because it was he who saved. This was not egocentricity in the ordinary sense. He calmly assumed that all this was true

[8] 1 Peter 2: 22.
[9] John 6: 35.
[10] See John 6: 28, 29; 8: 12; 14: 6.

and that if only people would come to him he could meet their need. It is well summarized in this call: 'Come to me, all who labour and are heavy laden, and I will give you rest. Take my yoke upon you, and learn from me; for I am gentle and lowly in heart, and you will find rest for your souls. For my yoke is easy, and my burden is light.'[11]

When the authorities sent officers to arrest him as he was teaching in the temple they returned empty-handed, saying hopelessly, 'No man ever spoke like this man.' They couldn't bring themselves to lay hands on him and lock him up.

Was he right?

It is no wonder that we read that 'there was a division among the people over him'. Some said he was mad, some said he was a deceiver and others accepted him as the divine Messiah. The influence of Christ in history makes it almost impossible to believe that he was a deceiver. His moral influence for uprightness, honesty and justice, is unequalled. He gladly died for his teaching. Besides, it is quite inconsistent with his whole character and teaching to think of him as a deceiver. If he was really deliberately deceiving others and at the same time giving this kind of teaching and example he must have been mad. But there is no category of madness known which allows a man to be at once a megalomaniac, believing that his life and death are the key to understanding the whole universe, and at the same time humble and the world's greatest influence for good. We cannot really say that he was mentally unhinged; yet what sane man could believe these things of himself if they were not true? No madman has ever had such an influence for making others sane and transforming society and individuals for good. If we are not able to accept him as God incarnate we have to find some other category. That is not at all easy. If he had merely been a great teacher we might say that, although he had great insight, he failed to have insight into himself. But, as we have seen, the fact is that his whole

[11] Matthew 11: 28–30.

teaching centred on himself. If he was wrong here he was totally wrong – and yet in so very many things of great importance there is no doubt that he was right.

We are not suggesting that our inability to find an alternative proves that he was right. We are simply saying that we need to watch our own honesty here. If we agree that he and his disciples claimed so much then we cannot lightly push it aside if we have no alternative explanation. Most people get around the problem by talking about Jesus as a moral teacher and conveniently forgetting the rest. That is not facing the data honestly. The dilemma needs to be faced. We need to let the data come to us afresh and try to ask ourselves honestly who he was.

11. Jesus' death and after

The meaning of the cross

The meaning that Jesus and his disciples gave to his death illustrates in a nutshell the dilemma in which his hearers found themselves. To Jesus his death was the climax and the chief purpose of his coming. Ludicrous as it may seem at first, he saw his death as epitomizing the whole relationship between God and man. His death created the 'new covenant'. The only kind of religious service that he actually commanded his disciples to continue was the memorial of his death in the Communion service.

This, however, is altogether understandable when we realize how he viewed his death. He said it was for the forgiveness of sins; and it was to forgive, and so bring men to fellowship with God, that he had come. He repeatedly stressed that he came to save sinners. That is to say, he came not merely to give the best advice on how to live or to order society. He did that incidentally, of course. But he really came to 'take away the sins of the world'. This is probably the most consistent and often repeated theme of the New Testament. Alongside the deity of Christ nothing else so excited the early Christians and nothing else was so central in their preaching and teaching as the fact that 'Christ died for our sins'.

To Nicodemus Jesus had compared the efficacy of his death to that of the brass serpent in the wilderness. That particular analogy explains that his death brought entirely free and unearned forgiveness. It does not explain how his death could alter the relationship between God and men. Other New Testament ways of talking about it do that. Jesus for instance called his forthcoming death 'a ransom'. In the Old Testament, as today, that was a price paid to buy someone out of bondage or out of some other predicament. But two other figures dominate the scene. Jesus' death is seen as the fulfilment of the Old Testament sacrifices and also of the prophecies of the suffering servant of Isaiah. In both cases the idea is of an innocent victim taking the punishment due to another. Forgiveness by God is seen as possible only when the sin has been punished – when justice has been done. The staggering claim of Jesus and the complete consensus of New Testament writers is that he was 'the Lamb of God, who takes away the sin of the world'; that 'he himself bore our sins in his body on the tree . . . By his wounds you have been healed'.[1]

Now there are three essential points here. First, the claim involved is completely nonsensical if Jesus was not himself divine. As Paul puts it in the explicit context of telling us about Christ's death for our sins, 'In Christ God was reconciling the world to himself, not counting their trespasses against them'.[2] The whole, great, New Testament theme of forgiveness, justification by faith, and mercy because our sins have been carried away by Christ is an impossible piece of wishful thinking if Christ is not so much more than man, more even than perfect man, that his death could atone for the sins of the world. 'There was no other good enough to pay the price of sin.' There was also no other great enough but God himself to do it.

Secondly, we drastically distort Jesus' picture of his own significance if we fail to think of him as not only the supreme revelation of God but also as the one who saves us from our sins and offers reconciliation to God through his death.

Thirdly, we can hardly understand certain events surrounding his death in any other way. He has inspired great numbers of Christians to die cheerfully for their faith in him. Many have undergone frightful tortures for him. Many have suffered bravely, though usually in a different spirit, for other causes. But Jesus himself faced his own death with

[1] John 1: 29; 1 Peter 2: 24.
[2] 2 Corinthians 5: 19.

horror. This fact would hardly have been recorded if it wasn't true, but the disciples record that he pleaded with God, 'Father, if thou art willing, remove this cup from me; nevertheless not my will, but thine, be done.'[3] We are told that being in an agony while he prayed his sweat became as great drops of blood falling down upon the ground. Further, on the cross itself he did not enjoy the unclouded assurance of God's smile, as so many Christian martyrs have done, including Stephen only a year or so later. At one point he called out, 'My God, my God, why hast thou forsaken me?'[4] We are told that at that time there was darkness over all the land. The disciples, who were taught by Jesus how to understand the events both before his death and after his resurrection, were not embarrassed to record these facts frankly, because to them they only showed an aspect of the horror of soul of the sinless Jesus when he took upon him the sins of the world and bore its punishment. Facts which one would have thought could almost completely discredit Jesus, they record unashamedly. This is the only real explanation.

We can summarize it all in terms of the great description of Jesus himself with which we began this section – 'full of grace and truth'. Jesus' death represents God's totally undeserved forgiveness and mercy (that is grace) but also it represents truth. God did not just pat us on the back and tell us to try better next time. His forgiveness was accomplished in such a way as not only to recognize the seriousness of sin and evil but even to make it plainer than ever before. The horror of evil and the truth that God must punish and destroy it is nowhere plainer than at the cross. Only there in fact do we dare to speak of it frankly, because there is the corresponding fact of God's even greater grace. That is probably why it is in connection with his death that Jesus and his disciples spoke of the glory of Jesus being fully shown. As Judas went out to betray Jesus and his death became imminent and certain, Jesus said to the remaining eleven, 'Now is the Son of man glorified, and in him God is glorified.'[5]

[3] Luke 22: 42.
[4] Matthew 27: 46.
[5] John 13: 31.

106

The antagonism of Judas

The histories of Judas Iscariot and of Thomas bring out the contrasting reactions to Jesus' death and resurrection. Judas was one of the twelve most intimate disciples. He was sent out with the others to preach and to heal. We have no indication that he was in any way different from the others in outward activity, because none of them seems to have suspected that he would be the betrayer. Jesus alone knew from the start. Although we are not told how he knew, we have some indication that Judas' whole attitude to Jesus was wrong, and that is something Jesus would have noticed as no-one else would. He must have admired Jesus' teaching; he was willing to preach and heal in Jesus' name; but the thing that really seems to have offended him most was the idea that Jesus had come to die. Judas had other tasks for Jesus to fulfil, probably social, military and political tasks. And when it became clear that Jesus was not going to fit into Judas' ideas, Judas became first dishonest (he stole from the common purse) and finally secretly hostile. Then he went to the authorities to ask how much they would pay him if he would betray Jesus.

The point is that Judas, while he probably accepted most of Jesus' moral teaching, was driven gradually into more and more definite antagonism to Jesus personally, just as the others were driven to more and more definite trust and obedience. Judas was even insensitive to Jesus' special token of love at the last meal they had together. He betrayed Jesus with a kiss, and when it was all over was filled with futile remorse. He went and threw down the money he had been given for the betrayal in front of those who paid it and then hanged himself.

Judas is not an un-modern character and he prompts the question as to how far the sense of the emptiness of life that is a feature of our twentieth-century culture is the result of a similar refusal to respond to God's loving revelation. Judas was driven to utter despair. Having rejected Jesus he found himself with nothing. How far is the present-day sense of meaninglessness the result of trying to live without God and finding that we have destroyed what gives meaning to life?

Jesus had that sort of effect on people. Either they came to a real faith or they had to fight him off, repudiate his claim and become part of the opposition. Neutrality became more and more difficult as people got to know him better. It was not only that Jesus' teaching clearly implied that one must trust and obey wholeheartedly, or not at all. Considering who he was and what he had come to do, that was inevitable; and today, as then, people tend to be pushed one way or the other.

Doubt gives way to faith

In spite of all this it was not until after his resurrection that the disciples came to a mature faith. They had so little understood his teaching that, when he was killed, they were for a while overwhelmed with doubt and despair. Thomas, one of the twelve, had not been present when Jesus first appeared to the disciples after his death. When they told him of it he replied that he would not believe unless he could actually touch the body and feel the nail prints and the spear wound in Jesus' side. Eight days later, Jesus again appeared to the inner circle and this time Thomas was present. He addressed himself directly to Thomas and invited him to carry out the experiment he had insisted would be necessary: 'Put your finger here . . . and do not be faithless, but believing.' Thomas, so confronted, did not need to do any experiments. He could see it was Jesus alive again and he fell at his feet with words of faith and worship, 'My Lord and my God!'[6]

We need to stop and think what it means that Thomas called him 'my God'. At last he also realized who Jesus was and trusted him with an unqualified commitment. It would seem that all his knowledge of Christ's life and teaching and character suddenly fell into place. As we have tried to show in this book, that is how faith usually comes – when a series of different reasons for faith are seen to fit together and

[6] John 20: 24–29.

create an absolutely convincing whole. It need not come in a flash, as it did to Thomas. But he was convinced. There was no further need for arguments or experiments. It all focused, however, not in a train of arguments, not in a theory, but in the person of Jesus. Now Thomas knew God he responded in the only possible way – in worship and obedient faith.

Jesus, however, made a comment that we need to remember. 'Have you believed because you have *seen* me? Blessed are those who have not seen and yet believe.' Thomas had not needed, as he thought, to touch and handle; but he had seen. Most Christians do not have such a privilege, and faith depends on neither physical sight nor touch. To us faith is the response to what we know about him and to the conviction that he is all he claimed to be. Like Thomas, however, we have to be sure that Jesus is not just a figure of history but a living reality today, and this leads us on to the next section of this book.

For many today the position is very like that of Thomas before this incident. They know a good deal about Jesus. They are at least inwardly aware of being faced by God in his creation and it seems very likely that Jesus is God incarnate as he claimed. They hang between faith and doubt, postponing decision until they are more sure. To such Jesus does not appear visibly as he did to Thomas. Today we have instead the opportunity of seeing the living impact of Christ in other people and the opportunity not only of reading the life of Jesus in the Gospels but of knowing that he rose from the dead and is alive today. This is the topic of Part III.

This discussion can do little justice to the wonder of the person of Christ. It is only too easy to brush him aside if we do not honestly face the data. If we do try sincerely to discover who he is, he pushes us along, as he did the disciples, to a personal faith in himself which sooner or later has to be declared openly. We are aware that he makes demands of us and that he has a right to do so because of who he is. Like Thomas, we find ourselves confronted by the living Christ whom we realize we must serve and worship as our Lord and our God.

Part Three
The living God

12. God is not dead

It would be possible to accept most of what I have said so far but still to have no personal Christian faith. You may agree that there is a Creator God behind everything. You may agree that Jesus Christ was divine in some sense and is a final revelation of God. But all that is long ago. What, you may ask, has it got to do with me personally?

The New Testament is very positive about this. It declares, first, that Jesus rose again and is alive today, and secondly that, though he is no longer physically present with us, he is present by his Spirit. The living reality of God has always been an actual experience to the Christian. It is subjective, in that we do not see, hear or feel anything physically. But God is a transforming reality in the everyday world. We are talking about the *living* God today, not some merely intellectual concept or some remote force. He is the God with whom *we* have to do. Here, too, there is evidence for the truth of Christianity in that it is still today a personal relationship with God.

If, then, we are asking for reasons for faith, the Bible leads us also to look at the effect of Christian faith in the lives of personal Christians and in the Christian community. Critics of Christianity have every right to ask searching questions here, and once more there is the danger of losing the wood for looking at the trees. But although the reasons for faith under this heading are much less strong on their own than in the other sections, they are important if we are to complete the picture. Christianity must be able at least to stand up to its critics in this area. In fact a great many people who have become Christian have started to be really interested in Christianity because of something that they have seen in the lives of Christians. By itself that could not be expected to bring anyone to faith but it has made them realize that, after all, Christianity could be true and that has driven them back to a fresh study of the person of Jesus Christ.

The resurrection of Jesus Christ is the bridge between the Gospels and the present experience of the Christian. When Jesus died the disciples were completely demoralized. Although Jesus had repeatedly told them that he would be killed like this, and that he would rise again, the reality of it was too much for them to take in. To start with they had all forsaken him and run away. That was bad enough. But in addition it was one of their own number who had actually betrayed him; and even Peter, one of his closest followers, had three times denied that he was a disciple. They must have been deeply ashamed of themselves and crushed in spirit.

But over and above that, Jesus had gone. The person in whom their faith and hope had rested was now dead. It seemed that they had lost all that really mattered because their faith was not just an acceptance of his teaching but a trust in him personally. In many religions and philosophies the death of the founder is not very crucial. What he has taught is far more important than what he is. But for Christianity that was not so. If Christ had simply died like other men and disappeared from the scene, that would have knocked the bottom out of the disciples' faith, proved that a considerable part of Christ's teaching was wrong, and left only a residue of ethical and theological instruction.

Yet within a few weeks the disciples were boldly declaring that Jesus was alive, though no longer visible; that he would be the judge of all men, so that men would have to deal with him one day; and that he had now come back in his Holy Spirit to live and work in the lives of all who would receive him. The argument of the first great sermon given by any of the disciples is instructive.[1] Peter on this occasion did

[1] See Acts 2.

not argue for the truth of the resurrection; he simply stated it as a fact of experience. But he then went on to argue that it was what anyone should have expected if they had realized who Jesus was: 'It was not possible for him to be held by death.' He reminded the audience that they knew enough about Jesus to realize that truth, though the disciples were also witnesses to the event. He called on them to recognize the phenomena that they heard and saw in the lives of the disciples as the work of the living Spirit of Christ. God, he said, is now active in the lives of ordinary disciples, as He promised. Jesus is alive. That is why you see and hear what you do. He rose from the dead. And he has given his Holy Spirit to transform us.

The evidence for the fact of the resurrection has often been spelt out and there are excellent modern treatments easily available.[2] It has been called the best attested fact in history, though that seems in some ways an exaggeration. But what is supremely attested is that the historical Jesus Christ was an amazing power in the lives of men years after his death. That implies the fact of his resurrection and, if we study it, it is hard to avoid the evidence for it. But it is not so much the fact that a miracle happened around the year AD 33. We could be persuaded of that and still not realize its relevance. The chief reason that the disciples spoke so often about it was that Jesus was alive and *with* them again. That was what restored the whole essence of their faith. Faith could be once more a trust and friendship with the personal, living Christ. What is more, the resurrection also confirmed what they had known, but perhaps doubted when he died, that he is the *divine* Saviour. He had overcome even sin and death and so was unmistakably marked out as the Son of God with power.

Certainly something suddenly transformed the disciples from a timid, discouraged and defeated little group into a band of intrepid evangelists whose enemies soon afterwards described them as 'those who have turned the world upside down'. We have to account for that transformation. Their

[2] See, *e.g.*, J. N. D. Anderson, *The Evidence for the Resurrection* (IVP, 1950); Michael Green, *Man Alive!* (IVP, 1967).

own explanation is that it was because they met the living Christ, at first physically present again after his resurrection for a few weeks, and then present in them when the Holy Spirit was given. The Holy Spirit, they realized, was Jesus' Spirit, and they speak interchangeably both of 'the Spirit within them' and of 'Christ within them' – as Jesus had done. They explained their experience as the activity of the living God in their lives. In terms of what we have said in earlier chapters this means that God is the living God in the world of men, as well as the Creator of all and the historically incarnate Saviour.

13. The living God in history

If God is the living God, who works in the lives of men, then there ought to be certain results that we can see in the past and present. History ought to show some clear evidence that Christianity is true or at least that it *could* be true. Yet we all know that the history of 'the church' is far from being an unqualified argument for Christianity. Indeed it seems to some people to be a very strong argument against it. We must therefore comment on the criticisms that are raised by any impartial study of the last two thousand years. It is the author's conviction that history is in fact not nearly as ambiguous in its evidence as a superficial reading might suggest. History does bear out the Christian's claims, but one reason for the difficulty is a failure to see what Christianity is and what sort of effect it could therefore be expected to have in historical terms.

Where the real evil lies?

First of all we must stress that Christ's teaching was not primarily social. It had, and has, enormous consequences for society. But he addressed himself primarily to the problem of the individual because that is where the great evils arise and that is where they must first be put right. This is not to decry social applications of Christianity. They are an essential task of the church. But they arise chiefly, though not exclusively, at the second stage when there are personal Christians to get on with the job of living the Christian life in the world. Many modern philosophers start the other end. They believe that, if only we could improve the environment, we should solve our social problems. The new society would produce new men free from the grosser evils which are said to arise from a bourgeois, competitive society, from the Corporate State (either Capitalist or Marxist) or from a possessive, 'nuclear' family, or whatever else is the particular *bête noire* of the philosophy concerned. If only this evil social influence could be removed, and a wholesome one put in its place, we are told, all would be well. Unfortunately the desired Utopia has never been achieved. We are always in an unfortunate 'transitional stage' and are told that we must not judge too quickly or harshly the efforts to reach a better society.

No-one will want to deny the bad effects of a bad environment. The New Testament, in fact, repeatedly stresses it. We are all aware of many evil influences in society today which must be fought and if possible overcome. But Jesus started at the other end. He taught that the real evil is in individual men and women and that unless we attack that we shall accomplish very little. For this reason he also taught that it is not altogether curable in this life. The evil is too deep seated. It could not be eliminated without destroying our humanity. Like some diseases the trouble is too pervasive and the necessary surgery would be fatal. Jesus even taught that the Christian would continue to find evil in his own nature. He did not promise to eliminate it – except after death. He offered to subdue it and to transform our characters progressively, but did not hold out the expectation that the individual Christian or the church would fully measure up to his ideals. The Christian is left looking forward to a completely re-structured new heaven and new earth in which there is the absolute rule of righteousness. Then evil will be eliminated even from our natures. Meanwhile the best of men is all too obviously imperfect.

In this sense the Christian gospel is like a doctor treating an arthritic old lady. It is no good his saying to her that he has a cure that will make her as lively as she was at the age of 30. He has no such thing and he knows it. He can only promise some relief of pain, some reduction of symptoms, some *degree* of improvement. The body has become old and marred, and many of these changes are irreversible. Those who offer sudden or complete cures are quacks. However well-meaning and sincere they may be, they deceive the patient – and they do so partly because they do not know enough medicine.

Evil in the church

If Jesus did not offer to make individuals perfect in this life, his promises with regard to the church are perhaps even more disappointing to the idealist. He repeatedly warned us that the church as an organization would be mixed. There would be plenty of people in the Christian community who were not real Christians. Wheat would be mixed with tares, the sheep would need to be separated from the goats at the judgment, though both were professing Christians. Even in apostolic times, when the church was small and socially unimportant, people joined it for wrong reasons and sought power in it for unworthy motives.[1] Jesus explained this situation by saying that any attempt to weed out all false Christians in this life would remove too much genuine, though weak, Christianity that was growing into something strong.

Whenever the church has been popular, wealthy, or powerful there have been special reasons for people who are not true Christians to get in on its organization. From the day when Constantine made Christianity the official religion of the Roman Empire, the temptations have been overwhelming for some. Of course the church should have fought back more vigorously and driven out of office those who had no right to be there. But throughout its history the church has been extremely mixed in its leadership as well as in its ordinary membership and this Jesus himself foresaw.

Even in Jesus' own band of disciples one out of the twelve was never a true believer, though he managed to live a life

[1] See Matthew 7: 13–25; Acts 8: 18.

outwardly the same as all the others and presumably, like the others, to preach fairly acceptably as a disciple. Jesus allowed Judas to be a disciple even though he knew that he was a betrayer, and many who are not true Christians have been allowed to be church officers with far less reason. We cannot altogether blame Christianity for its hypocrites any more than we blame a hospital for its patients. We do blame the hospital, however, if its patients do not on the average get a lot better. The church has often been too comprehensive, especially when people have tried to make it coterminous with the nation. But its members, whether they are genuine Christians or not, are still sinners and will never be completely healed of their moral sickness as long as they live. The history of the very best churches, therefore, is not, and could not be, an altogether clean record. Sin is too intractable in the Christian for that. Nevertheless it should be a record of real good accomplished. What we have to ask is, Has Christianity made people better than they would otherwise be in a way that matches its claims? Obviously they are far from perfect and the church is even further from being perfect.

What does Christianity offer?

Christianity is therefore a disappointment to many social reformers. Not only does it not offer the kind of solution hoped for, it pours scorn on many of the solutions of others and says that they are raising false hopes. Yet the Utopians of the political left, right and middle, and those who have given up politics and look for a Utopia of another kind, will continue to feel cheated. They feel that Christianity ought to offer a better Utopia on earth than they offer. They complain that the refusal to offer an alternative is only a wangle to get out of the church's failures. In fact, however, taking the view of human nature that the Christian does take, no Utopia is possible[2] and Christians are wrong if they suggest that they have one to offer.

[2] See chapter 4 on the problem of evil.

Because Christians know what they do know about the state of humanity they can expect only some *degree* of improvement in human beings and some *degree* of improvement of society as a result. To start by trying to improve society results in relatively little progress because the real disease is untouched. Some social gains can be achieved that way, but men remain as fundamentally miserable with themselves even in the improved order, so that the benefits prove disappointing. To continue the analogy of the medical doctor: he has to treat the disease, but at the same time he must try to deal with the worst symptoms (pain, *etc.*). He is heartless if he does nothing about pain until the disease is cured. But if he tackles only the symptoms one by one, the disease will produce new symptoms soon after the first have been overcome. You do not have to be a Christian in order to tackle some of the symptoms. Only the Christian message, however, really deals with the disease. Christians are therefore bound to concentrate on that radical cure even if the result is that many people turn to Utopian quacks who promise cures that they cannot accomplish.

For those who are not Utopian, however, there is still plenty of ammunition with which to attack the church. But the criticisms are very varied and sometimes cancel one another out. Therefore, rather than try to answer them in turn, we will try to set out briefly the Christian's positive view of the matter.

According to the teaching of Christ the real trouble with man is his wrong relationship to God. Having turned away from God, who should be the centre of his life, he has become first preoccupied and then blinded by secondary goals (or ideals) of various kinds. These may be good as far as they go, but they cannot stand in for God. Some men and women are purely self-interested, of course. But those who are not are still serving lesser and competing deities, whether they are material entities, such as money, or a class, or nation, or culture, or abstract ideals. Becoming a Christian never does away completely with all that, as we have said; but it does radically change our orientation.

Genuine Christian experience brings us to a right relationship to God – a new inner life in fellowship with him. This involves a re-ordering of our whole life. If people are genuine Christians then God is once more the centre of life. That is what is meant by repentance and faith – a turning from old ideas to God and a 'trust and obey' relationship to him. That change of fundamental orientation has all sorts of repercussions as it is worked out in life. It should be the sort of change that leads us to believe it is a work of God rather than simply a change of philosophy. Personal ambition and satisfaction immediately lose some of their power for instance. But they do not suddenly disappear, neither are they suddenly completely integrated with the love of God which is Christ's first commandment, or the love of men which is his second commandment. There is a fundamental change, but it works out gradually.

The result is that no Christian should ever believe that he himself, or other Christians, is either perfect or impervious to temptation. Really this ought to be so obvious as not to need saying, but non-Christians keep on thinking that Christians profess to be above evil and selfish attitudes or deeds, and that every lapse from perfection is therefore an argument against Christianity. What would be an argument against Christianity would be a situation in which becoming a Christian did not make a positive and noticeable difference *in degree* for good. This ought to be visible on the scale of history and particularly so since Christians profess not only to have been re-orientated by becoming Christians, but to have an experience of God's continuing work in their lives. Christ, it is said, 'lives in your hearts by faith'. The result therefore ought to be some real degree of Christ-likeness even if it has not yet worked out in terms of its full personal and social implications.

The social results of Christianity should be expected in two main areas. First, there is the impact of individual Christians on their society. Secondly, there is the effect of Christian teaching on society as a whole. Before trying to argue positively, however, it must be said that Christians have cause for deep shame concerning many things done in the name of Christianity and even many things done by people professing personal Christian faith. If, in what follows, we seem to be stressing the positive side, it is not because we are complacent but because these things are true and ought to be said also. Criticisms of Christianity abound; the positive side is not so often heard.

Christianity's effects on individuals

We all know of some of the heroes of the Christian faith. Men and women have been transformed by the Christian message from being selfish, anti-social and miserable into people who have served others sacrificially and have joyfully suffered all kinds of hardships for the faith. The blood of the martyrs and pioneer missionaries has been the seed of the churches, not least because they showed such a quality of character that observers were deeply impressed. The Roman persecution of the Christians, for instance, did much to spread Christianity because the public saw how they died and how they had lived. It would be easy to quote great examples. But it would also be unfair if one did not at the same time admit that there had been famous Christians who, apparently because of their faith, did terrible things. There have been blind fanatics and worse, though we can see that they were far from the teaching and spirit of the Bible.

But, even though the other side of the story must be faced, we have to admit that very remarkable things have happened in individual lives when people have become Christian. Many, many people have been rescued from degradation; many homes have been transformed when the father or mother has been converted; many societies have been reformed by Christian leaders; many of the greatest noble deeds have come from a Christian motivation. This does not necessarily make us want to be Christian. Often the cost and the discipline that were involved put us off. But there is little doubt that there is ground for thankfulness for what was done and for admiration for the inward change that made it possible.

Christianity's social effects

Similarly, there can be no doubt that in a very great many parts of the world the influence of the church has proved a colossal impetus to almost all that is good, though this influence has never been faultless. There have been foul wars, persecutions and other evils perpetrated by, or supported by, the church's institutional leaders. But, on the other hand, it must be said that hospitals and health services, schools and universities, the battle against bribery and corruption, social welfare, the raising of the position of women, a sense of the responsibility of society to children, to other races, to the weak and deprived and many other social advances, owe a large part of their origin and early impetus to Christian influences. Some intellectuals speak as if it was not Christians who advanced learning, founded universities and schools, developed science and medicine, the professional ideal of service for others, and many other things we now take for granted.[3] By now the ideas have been secularized and some of them taken over by atheists; but at least we should recognize that Christianity has had many influences for undoubted good on a huge scale. The picture is much more positive than many people will admit. Now when, for lack of Christianity, some of these things are in danger (*e.g.* the ideal of public service) we begin to realize how much we stand to lose. To take an example; during the time of Hitler's power practically no-one stood up to Hitler in Germany itself except certain groups of Christians. Many Christians did not oppose as they should, but the intellectual and cultural leadership of the universities and other institutions hardly raised a whisper, and it was left almost entirely to the 'confessing church' to make a protest. Christianity proved more powerful than learning and culture in giving men courage and determination to stand up for what was right.

It is impossible to draw up a balance sheet, but let us acknowledge that many of the dirty and tough jobs of

[3] See, *e.g.*, R. Hooykaas, *Religion and the Rise of Modern Science* (Scottish Academic Press, 1972 and Open University Textbook, 1973).

service to the needy have been done by Christians because of their Christian faith. Who runs the leprosy hospitals even today? What body can show a record that will bear comparison with that of the Salvation Army, the great missionary societies in their medical and educational work, and the unobtrusive social service of the Christian ministry?

It has to be said that those who have accomplished most socially were also usually those who put the gospel before social service. Just because they were personal Christians they were heavenly minded; but they cared for the this-worldly condition of men in more practical and effective ways than those who emphasized only social service. Usually the latter asked the Government to go and 'do something'. The gospel enthusiasts certainly had their weaknesses. Perhaps they too rarely put pressure on others (such as Governments) to act. But at least they got on and did something *themselves* while others talked, and they also have a far from negligible record of solid achievements in lasting institutions, wholesome cultures and improved Government in many directions.

This discussion has so far not raised the question of whether there is a particularly Christian political programme. There are plenty of people of all political schools who believe that Christianity ought to be on their side, and Christians ought indeed to be in favour of whatever policies will increase righteousness, justice, mutual care and the other social virtues that they prize highly. We are told to pray to this effect, which shows both that God cares and that we ought to care also. But we cannot say that Christians have been able to reach a consensus as to what political and economic policies are dictated by those shared ideals. Certainly there is no biblical blue-print as to what political policy is best calculated to achieve the Christian aims. The answer is, perhaps, that at different times in history different methods are needed – as the Communist theorists also agree. If so we should not be too shocked when institutionalized Christianity seems often to be tied to the political methods of a past generation. It has been said that if Christianity is wedded to the culture of one generation it will be widowed in the next. This, alas, has often happened. Society changes so fast that we have to try to think out afresh in each generation what political methods are best calculated to forward Christian ideals for it. If people complain that the Bible ought to give more guidance than that, it must be replied that the Bible does not even give a blue-print for the church, let alone for secular society. Christian conduct is not meant to be the application of blue-prints to life but a sensitive and loving application of principles. The best kind of state structure (and church structure) may vary greatly in relation to the actual situation.

One very interesting and important point emerges from the study of this history. On the whole it is those Christians who have taken the Bible most seriously who have accomplished most. The Reformation, for instance, represented a dramatic change towards a more definitely Christian influence in society and in personal life. And this was basically because the pulpits were filled by men who set themselves to preach the Bible and the ordinary man was encouraged and enabled to read the Bible for himself. If one is examining and criticizing movements and individuals of the past it is always significant to ask how far their life was really moulded by the Bible rather than by other nominally Christian traditions. The Bible-based revivals and missions, such as the Methodist revival and the nineteenth-century evangelical missions, remoulded society in ways that represent a great advance in social righteousness and harmony in personal and family enrichment and 'health'. We can now see some of their mistakes, but the Christians of this school brought about astonishing progress because they were nearer to original Christianity.

None of these movements or individuals was perfect. For instance the group of evangelical Christians who led and carried through the abolition of the slave trade, and finally of slavery itself, also had their blind spots like others. It is fashionable today to try to debunk Wilberforce because at one stage he voted against the Reform Bill. But who in his generation had achieved anything like so much for humanity at home and abroad? And how can we explain his positive achievements if we do not, as he did, attribute it to an evangelical conversion – that is, to the entrance of the power of God in new life and totally new values? We must not indulge in unrealistic hagiography. We must paint these men 'warts and all'.[4] But when we do so we see even more clearly the wonder of God's work in the lives of men who were by no means perfect, but alarmingly like ourselves.

Such historical judgments are notoriously difficult. Some sections of the community left better records than others and, in any case, this book is not the place to go into the matter thoroughly. What we can say without fear of contradiction is that genuine Christian faith often did produce a striking degree of concern for others, of unselfish service, of love, joy, peace, and the other virtues that the New Testament says are the signs of genuine Christianity. We may not admire these Christ-like qualities. If we are Fascists, for instance, we may despise them. But Christianity does not profess to produce good Fascists, or good bullies, or violent revolutionaries, or good 'drop-outs', or a number of other characters that are admired by some today. Christianity professes to produce a particular kind of influence and there is plenty of evidence that it has done so.

[4] It was Oliver Cromwell who insisted, when his portrait was being painted, that the artist do it as it was – 'warts and all'. It is a pity that this realism, like the Bible's realism when it describes its heroes, has not always been the rule in Christian biography and in Christian assessment of history.

14. Does the Christian way of life work?

There is, as we said, another level at which the matter can be discussed which depends less on historical judgment. If Christianity is true, the Christian way of life is given by God the Creator and is not only for a particular time two thousand years ago in the Middle East, but for all time and for all cultures. Can that claim be maintained? Is the Christian way the best way when it is truly lived out? Or perhaps we ought to ask, Would it be if it were truly lived out? Does it work?

The Christian claim is that, if people really live according to the teaching of Christ, this is far and away the best for society and for the individual. That is not to say that Christianity makes a man 'healthy and wealthy and wise' in terms of what society values. It is certainly not very likely to make him rich, and it will not necessarily make him a better scholar or a more 'successful' business man. The Christian claim is that Christian teaching is exactly fitted to man as he is in the world as it is. If, therefore, we follow it we can expect that our life will prove vastly more satisfactory *in terms of the ideals of Christianity*.

Not all Christians are leaders, or scholars, or free from physical and psychological illness. Certainly they have no reason to expect to be free from the ordinary troubles of men. Indeed, if the teaching of Christ and the apostles is taken seriously, they have reason to expect that in some ways they will fare worse. But the Christian way of life should commend itself as producing a certain wholeness or wholesomeness which enables Christians to be free in God's world.

By enjoying life in rightly directed ways they should get more into life than they otherwise would. Christians speak of God's service as 'perfect freedom' and that is genuinely meant, even if it is very imperfectly demonstrated. Christianity, it is claimed, is tailor-made for the actual situation of men in a very imperfect society. It is not for the monastery, or the non-existent ideal community of perfect people. It is for real life with our own and other people's shortcomings. It is for men and not for angels.

The Christian family ideal

If we take the example of the family the point may be clearer. The Christian believes in the ideal of stable, monogamous families where husband and wife live together in love, mutual respect and faithfulness, and in which parents love and take responsibility for their own children, and children accept the authority of their parents while they are young and give them honour throughout life. Whether such a family must be a 'nuclear' family as in Western Christendom, or could follow out other patterns such as the 'extended' family, is not fundamental. But that the features outlined above are New Testament teaching there is no doubt. The Christian says that this ideal is given by the Creator. It therefore corresponds not only to the way men and women ought to do things, but also to our nature, that is the way in which we were designed to do them. To live as we were created to live must be the best for us. It should therefore be possible to show that this sort of family brings benefits to mankind and that these benefits, or at least some of them, are of a purely human this-worldly nature. If so, we can judge them objectively.

The Christian ideal of the family might of course have spiritual benefits which the doubter would fail to appreciate. But if it is really the Creator's ideal, it should also fit our humanity so well that it is seen to be, from a purely humanitarian point of view, good, healthy, and constructive. The Christian cannot escape this debate by saying that he is

9

more concerned with spiritual than with social benefits. The Creator is, of course, more concerned with the spiritual, but he is also concerned with the this-worldly life of his creatures and, because he loves them, has given his law and his gospel for the present life – as well as to lead us to the life to come.

It is open to the advocates of Women's Lib for instance to disagree with the ideal. But then the critics of the Christian ideal must be willing to show, not merely that the Christian ideal has been abused in a largely non-Christian society where Christian motives have gone, or that it can, like every other relationship, become a cold formality. They must show that the ideal itself is wrong and is responsible for evils which will be remedied only if a new ideal is adopted. They must also show that the absence of life-long commitment to husband and children is of positive value to women, men and children, and to society as a whole. In fact, however, it has been almost universally believed that society gains when children are brought up in stable homes, and it is proving increasingly difficult to maintain such without a life-long living commitment of the parents. Those who attack the Christian ideal of the home have got to show that their alternative will work better in the long run.

One factor often misunderstood in this is that the Christian believes that the biblical ideal of the family is best, not only for unselfish and noble people, but for all. We believe, indeed, that it is even more necessary because men and women are sinful than it would be if they were perfect. Paul's comment on marriage, that it is far better than immorality, has often been misunderstood.[1] He does not advocate marriage merely as a defence against immorality. It is quite clear from other parts of his teaching that he had a very positive view of marriage. What he says here, and the point is important, is that for most people the alternatives are not nearly so good and are often positively evil. Life-long and faithful marriage is God's way of enabling imperfect men and women to put their God-given sexuality to an entirely wholesome and constructive purpose. Sex easily becomes

[1] 1 Corinthians 7. See the discussion of this passage in *Living and Loving* by A. N. Triton (IVP, 1972).

destructive – at least of other people. But God's plan is that it should become a creative bond between a man and his wife and help to bring into being the richest of all friendships and partnerships. Nothing elevates the position and honour of women in relation to men more than this, as can be seen by looking at the alternatives. Women's Lib are right when they protest at the degradation of womanhood that is a feature of depersonalized sex. But they are usually mistaken in the way they seek to remedy that situation and it is certainly not Christianity that is responsible for the pornography and vulgar advertisements to which, amongst other things, they so rightly object.

Today it seems to be widely recognized that the best way of providing psychological and social health for children is by a stable home in which the parents are truly loving to each other and to the children.[2] So often those who decry Christian standards start by saying that you cannot impose them on people who have been socially deprived. Deliquents should be helped to overcome the effects of their home deprivation. It thus emerges, however, that what they mean is that these people have been deprived of the healthful influence of Christian standards in their own home. If that is so it is by no means clear why they should not be helped, for the good health of the next generation, to provide what they themselves have lacked. They may be past the stage of being much helped by discipline or mere repetition of the moral law; but the ideal remains the same for them as for their parents.

There are many other aspects of the Christian ideal of family life and all could be discussed similarly. In each aspect we have no hesitation in claiming that the biblical principles, when applied in the spirit of the Bible, have obvious advantages for the partner and for society. We cannot 'prove' that they are best in a knock-down manner,

[2] Paul says that husbands should love their wives 'as Christ loved the church and gave himself up for her'. Love, he says, 'is patient and kind ... bears all things ... hopes all things, endures all things. Love never ends' (Ephesians 5: 25; 1 Corinthians 13: 4–8). He prefaces a discussion of the home with 'Be subject to one another' (Ephesians 5: 21).

because it depends on what in life is held to be of value. But they can stand up for themselves in the current debate with confidence as commending themselves to most people's consciences.

The family is only one example, but it is a good one because it is much discussed or researched; and the biblical view is clear and, on the whole, one that we would, for practical reasons, like others to follow even if we don't want to do so ourselves. Like every other ideal it can become a cold legalism and it most easily does so when it is stripped of all its Christian motives and becomes a mere set of rules. That has happened painfully often. But even then, when it is most legalistic and Pharisaical, it really is socially better than the alternatives. That is why countries like Russia, which at one time spoke of the family as a 'bourgeois' idea, have returned to a most puritanical family life for practical reasons. The alternatives were so much worse!

Many are urging today that the traditional Christian ideals for personal and social life should be liberalized or abolished. Sometimes this comes from the anti-Christian wing of the Humanist movement; sometimes, as with much of the agitation regarding Sunday restrictions, from commercial interests. There may be a great variety of motives and philosophies behind the opposition and no doubt most of it is based on a sincere belief that some alternatives would be better. What is proposed as an alternative, however, is hardly ever anything that has actually been lived out, except by a tiny minority dependent (and sometimes parasitic) upon a society ordered in a loosely Christian way. When most people tell the truth dishonest men can flourish. When most homes are stable, society can cope with the debris of a proportion of broken homes. The Christian believes that in every aspect of it the Christian way of life is in fact the best for society and that, although this cannot be proved absolutely – because in this area nothing can be proved – there is a good deal of experience to show that that claim is valid.[3] This is not to argue that Christianity should be ac-

[3] See the chapter 'Are Christian morals for all men?' in *Whose World?* by A. N. Triton (IVP, 1970).

cepted because it is practically helpful. It is rather that, because Christian ethics show such a remarkable 'fit' for the life of all men, we have another reason to believe that the Christian claims are true.

The ten commandments

One could argue the matter similarly in relation to other aspects of the ten commandments, or of the New Testament lists of practical do's and don'ts which arise out of them. The Christian emphasis on truth, for instance, has had incalculable benefits when it has been lived out, and the tremendous stress on justice, although it has been so little obeyed, has transformed most of the societies into which it has come.

Of course many of these biblical ideals seem rather obvious to non-Christians. At least that is true in countries where they have been tried out in the past. Non-Christians now rightly say that you don't have to be a Christian to believe in truth and justice and that some non-Christians always have believed in them quite independently of the Judaeo-Christian tradition. That is true and in fact what we are arguing is that Christian morals are so perfectly related to the real situation of men that every aspect of them should be, if not obvious, at least capable of good practical justification in the light of experience. The Christian does not profess that Christian ethics are entirely original. Wise men had worked out some of it before. What the Christian claims is that Christian morals *as a whole* are the best, that no aspect of them is at fault, and that the more they have been followed, the healthier society has been and the more truly free and healthy individuals have become.

It is not logical to dismiss the Christian way of life as in part obvious to the non-Christian and for the rest fallacious. The Christian way of life was not obvious at all when it was first promulgated. Now we see overwhelming reasons for some of it and tend to reject the rest as too troublesome. The Christian replies that it is a package deal. Much of it is now accepted by non-Christians because it has proved itself. The same would be true of the rest if only we worked it out fully.

That is a very big claim and in the nature of the case it is virtually impossible either to prove or to disprove it in any complete sense. What does need to be argued today is that Christian morals, far from being a hindrance to the highest developments of our humanity and of our society, are in fact entirely compatible with these aims, and that they can be shown to have a very good claim to have been the greatest force tending in that direction.

The trouble is partly that the purely negative aspects of the Christian ideal are the ones that remain as bare skeletons when the life has gone out of Christianity. If we forget that it was the Old Testament law that said 'Thou shalt love thy neighbour as thyself' and think only of the negative aspects of the ten commandments, we are distorting the picture. There are negative aspects to the Old Testament law, as there are to any system of laws, but their aim is constantly stated to be positive and the particular commands are only giving teeth to the great commandments, 'Thou shalt love the Lord thy God with all thy heart' and 'Thou shalt love thy neighbour as thyself'. Everyone approves at least of the latter. The question is, How do we best bring about that sort of community? The Christian answer is that we need first an inward change of heart and then we need to live according to Christian morals. That is the best way to get near to the ideal. The outline of these standards in the ten commandments as worked out by Jesus is more simple than people realize. It could be summarized as follows:

Respect and love for God and his Name (*i.e.*, his reputation).

One day in seven off work – a day for rest and worship.

Honour your parents and love your children.

No murder or injury to others.

Marital faithfulness and love and pre-marital chastity.

No theft. Justice in work relationships and the human dignity of work rather than idleness as a means to serving others.

Truth.

No greed or envy.

134

Our society in the West is increasingly marred by greed, violence, loss of truth, growing injustice and loss of respect for marriage, for parents, and for the need of others for a day of rest. No wonder it is not a happy or settled community. But the answer is as likely to be found in a return to these ideals and laws as in some new kind of norm. They have created enormous benefits in the past. By contrast the ideals could be independence of parents, children and family, violent revolution, sexual amorality (sometimes called freedom), no respect for truth or for other people's property (such as the environment of future generations), and the totally competitive society where everyone is for himself, or his clique, and the devil is left to take the hindermost. The prospect is spine-chilling both at the personal and social levels. Those who attack the ten commandments often forget what they actually command and what their opposites would be like.

This cannot be a conclusive argument. But we can say that Christian morality makes out a good case for itself. It is far from unreasonable to claim that it is the *Creator's* rule. It will not of course be easy to live out. It will make big demands on the individual. But the Christian life is compared to an athletic contest. The successful athlete who often performs with an appearance of extraordinary ease and delight is the one who has trained and keeps training, avoiding certain evils and insisting on certain positive things in his diet and way of life. By themselves the rules of training for sport look petty (no smoking, early bed, diet, much exercise, no alcohol, or very little, no drugs, *etc.*), but their aim is *positive* health. The same is true for Christian ethics. It is very plausible when we see the positive results. We may not like the negative aspect and may possibly not admire the results altogether, as we resent slightly the extremely fit man and call him 'disgustingly healthy'. But Christianity can more than stand up to its critics here, as others have argued much more fully. The Christian way of life does work and has worked in history.

15. The living God today

In the end, of course, we will settle this question, not by asking historical questions such as what happened in the sixteenth or seventeenth centuries when the Bible was released again amongst the people, nor by making general judgments about the Christian way of life, but by asking, What are Christians like today? This is not a question that can really be argued out on paper. We have to judge to a large extent by our own experience. What is important, however, is that we do not simply ask whether I like Christians or whether they would make good members of the sort of culture or society that I admire. They have a way of not fitting easily into too tight a community, for instance, since they have both a respect for individuality and also certain ethical standards which they insist upon. They would be bad members of some kinds of society of the right, left or centre. For example they would fit into only certain kinds of commune. They have a way of refusing some of the standards of both the middle and the working classes, and even more of the rich. And yet many of us became Christians, including the author, partly because there was something about some Christians which was sufficiently convincing to make us want to go into their faith very carefully indeed. We saw something that was not just the product of their human environment but seemed to demand explanation in terms of a work of the living God in their individual lives and in the community of believers.

One has to put alongside that statement the fact that many people say they are not Christians partly because of the way in which others professing Christianity have behaved towards them. Often they have genuine cause for complaint. Sometimes they are making excuses. Always we have to be willing to think again and ask ourselves whether there is not some reason to think that, in spite of their blatant imperfections, there are plausible tokens of a work of God in the lives of *some* who profess to have a relationship with God in Christ.

The individual is always difficult to judge in isolation. It is always possible that he was especially fortunate in his heredity and environment. After all some cats or dogs have 'nice' temperament. The Christian community, therefore, helps us to see what the individual alone makes less clear. It is not that there are features of the communal life that are impressive – that is another question which we are not discussing here. It is that people of all kinds of backgrounds and heredities acquire certain characteristics in common when they become Christians. Certain traits appear. There seems to be reality in many instances about their claim to be in relationship with God. He really does seem to be doing something in their lives and character, though they remain anything but complete and perfect. The point at issue is whether God has begun a work in them and started to transform them into the likeness of Christ in even a very small degree. We don't have to like Christians in order to acknowledge that here, in some way, God is at work. The living God has taken the most unlikely and often unattractive human material and begun to do something. This to many people is a fresh reminder that Christianity is true. It is often sadly distorted but, if only we could get at its central realities, we would see that here is a work of the living God.

How strong is the evidence?

Such evidence can never be conclusive. It can at best give us a hint of a new kind of reality which we must admit *could be* a purely psychological phenomenon. It can only help us to go back to the more objective data that we have discussed in the first two sections with a new openness of mind. It can make us admit that perhaps there is more to it than meets the eye and that we ought to ask again what is the true explanation of the world and of the person of Jesus Christ. The logic of this opening of our minds through the lives of Christians is similar to that discussed in Part I. Nature is not perfect, yet it bears witness to a perfect God. History is much more obscure and tentative. We may only be able to say that we think we have seen something. Perhaps, after all, there is more to life than matter in motion and these people have a small part of the secret of it. That is not because they are any better than others but because something seems to have happened to them. They say they have met God in Jesus Christ and it could be true. We must have another look for ourselves. As we look through history there are some scandalous things that shock us and which are difficult for Christians to explain; but there are plenty of individuals and movements that really do show signs of having been inspired by the living God. So it is in the lives of men and women to-day. Some show signs of being not only inspired by external ideals but inwardly empowered and motivated by God.

Some readers will say that they simply do not agree. They are entitled to their judgment. We can only ask them to think again and to consider that they may be wrong. We ourselves do see great cause for encouragement in the lives of many Christians of the past and present. We discover here fresh grounds for confidence in God and fresh hope for ourselves that what God did for them he can surely do for us, so that we in our day may be transformed to be far more consistently Christlike. Others may say they just do not see it. The Christian can only ask them to keep looking.

As we have said, this is a far weaker argument for Christianity than the much more objective evidence of the created order and even weaker still than the evidence of the life of Jesus Christ. The reason for this is easy to see. Whereas Jesus Christ was perfect and the natural order still shows many traces of its original perfection, man has an active principle of evil still within him and the plain devilishness of it is constantly cropping up and distorting the noblest aims. The

Christian of all people should be most aware of this. Indeed the greatest 'saints' have been the most conscious of their sin and humbled by it. The evidence adds up to something like the argument of Peter in his first great sermon which could be summarized as follows: 'These men are not drunk as you suppose (or deluded or demented) . . . but this phenomenon in their lives is part of the fulfilment of what Jesus Christ promised. If you know anything about him you will realize that he must be alive still, he must be active in the lives of his children and we shall all finally have to come to face him, because he is the living God.' Experience is a hint and a signpost to the reality of the Creator who makes himself known in Christ and is confronting us today as the living God.

Conclusion: Is faith reasonable?

Finally, and very briefly, is faith reasonable? We have tried to show that there are plenty of positive reasons that point toward faith. When all is said and done, however, the case is not proved. But then it is not the sort of case that can be proved. And if it were, the resulting 'faith' would be a sterile intellectual affair. Christian faith is faith in the living God. It is, therefore, a personal trust and is far more than just accepting certain theoretical truths. Faith is possible only when we have seen that God is really there and that he is all he claims. In the nature of the case, then, faith is not just the sort of thing that could be proved by pure logic. But it is not unreasonable. Indeed it is based on good reasons. It is reasonable in the sense that it makes uniquely good sense of reality. But if by being 'reasonable' we mean something that is the necessary end-point of a purely rational argument, then Christian faith is not that kind of thing. As we have said, many, if not most, of the really important decisions and relationships in life are not 'reasonable' in that narrow sense, but they are usually nevertheless reasonable in the broader sense that we can equally apply to faith. Those who believe are not going against reason or experience. On the contrary, our experience and reasoning about it edge us along constantly towards faith. The enemies of faith are not experience and reason but ignorance and a refusal to think about the facts. This conclusion – that faith is reasonable in this sense – is not, however, in itself enough. From that we have to go on to personal trust.

When it comes to the point our problem is that we do not

altogether follow reason. We may know that the Christian position is true and yet do nothing whatever about it. It is only when God brings this fact home to us with the kind of reality and force that so great a truth deserves that we are driven to trust. We often find ourselves holding back – especially when the trail seems hot. Even if we seek, we do not seek wholeheartedly. Here we discover some of our own dishonesty and no-one is always honest with demanding truths.

Different things form the last step in the process of coming to personal trust. No two people's experience is identical, as the New Testament examples show. But the substance of faith remains the same for all. When we have our eyes opened to realize that Jesus Christ is the personal presence of the living, Creator God, then the only right response is to trust him. That will involve a recognition that we have held him at arm's length, that our lack of faith has had large elements of rebellion in it and that we have to some extent suppressed the truth which we did know. But in Christ, and through his death, there is a way of return and forgiveness. The journey is one that is bound to be humiliating. It involves a recognition that we have been wrong as well as that our own cleverness is not enough to get on to the truth. There is both a moral and intellectual humiliation before we accept God's self-revelation and God's undeserved forgiveness. But one of the highest functions of reason is to discover its own limitations and its dependence on what is 'given'. Equally the beginning of true morality often lies in the discovery of our own deficiencies, including our pride. It is not easy to admit that we are intellectually and morally wrong and to come to God for the answer. But that is the way things really stand. It is sometimes even harder to accept from God his undeserved mercy and forgiveness. But there is no other way out.

Jesus Christ, as we have said, described himself as 'the way, and the truth, and the life'. If he is not all that, he remains the most astonishing and inexplicable person in history. If Jesus is not the *truth* about God, we still have to come up with some other explanation of the world. If Jesus is not the *way* to God, we still have to discover a way for ordinary mortals, with all their chronic sinfulness, to be forgiven and brought to personal fellowship with God. If Jesus is not the *life* we have to show that there is a better way. The three main parts of this book could have been classified under these three heads. It all focuses in Jesus Christ – the only full revelation of God. The Christian is one who has accepted this claim of Jesus as true and who has therefore trusted him personally. And if we trust him, then we are launched into the Christian way – making him in practice our Lord and our God.

Faith, therefore, is a different kind of thing from mere logic, but far from going against reason it is the response we have to make when we understand that Christ is all he claimed to be. Faith is the result of seeing how things really are. Once we see it we cannot escape from that understanding of reality. It is therefore entirely right to use all our abilities in order to seek understanding. It makes sense to ask God (if he is there) to give us understanding. Many people find that they can ask God, in this way, without begging the question. We want to know the truth so that we can live in accordance with it and not with a delusion. And God cares about truth. He could not possibly want us to believe a lie. We can therefore ask to be shown the truth.

What I have been doing in this small book is to try to help others to look at reality *in such a way* that they see what it is all about and believe and trust in Christ as a result. There are many other points that could have been raised. There are many other problems to which an answer could have been attempted. This book is meant to provide at least a starting point.

The next step should be to go back and read again any one of the Gospels as honestly as we can, seeking to see who Jesus Christ is. This book is all secondary material. It is intended to provide a stimulus to further thought and reading and discussion, and for that purpose the Gospels are the ideal source.

For further reading

Part 1

D. M. MacKay, *The Clockwork Image* (IVP, 1974).

J. W. Wenham, *The Goodness of God* (IVP, 1974).

Charles Martin, *How human can you get?* (IVP, 1973).

Part II

Leon Morris, *The Lord from Heaven* (IVP, 2nd ed., 1974).

J. N. D. Anderson, *Christianity: the Witness of History* (IVP, 1969).

Michael Green, *Jesus Spells Freedom* (IVP, 1972).

Part III

J. N. D. Anderson, *The Evidence for the Resurrection* (IVP, 1950).

Michael Green, *Man Alive!* (IVP, 1967).

A. N. Triton, *Whose World?* (IVP, 1970).

General

The New Testament!

J. R. W. Stott, *Basic Christianity* (IVP, 2nd ed., 1971).

J. R. W. Stott, *Becoming a Christian* (IVP, 1950).